CW00871025

To my long suffering wife Eula and the cadets of the 24th General Poananga cadet wing.
In memory of Sergeant Rodney 'Jacko' Edwards.

BIOLOGY & BOOGERS

I always wanted to be a Marine Biologist. I don't know why: I hate fish, science bores me stupid and I turn to jelly at the thought of diving.

As it turned out the marine biology fraternity was quite safe. My dreams of zipping around the seven seas in a rubber sea craft were crushed the day my School Certificate results were released. I got 32 for Biology. I was still 20-odd marks shy of even being allowed to drive the boat.

Time for a re-think.

On checking my marks I found I could rule out any profession that required mathematical aptitude or scientific flair. My spelling was dodgy, my geography left a lot to be desired and most of my reports featured the phrase 'Could try harder'. It was true: I could, but I didn't. The only subject I excelled at was history, but I was struggling to find a career where Garibaldi's liberation of Italy was relevant.

Nope, the only things I had in my favour were big feet, an honest nature and an overriding passion for the colour blue. It was going to be a toss-up between painting swimming pools and joining the police force.

The constabulary won, which was lucky because my painting skills left a lot to be desired. I told Mum and Dad the good news. At first they were crushed: they had their hearts set on my becoming a marine biologist. Dad was particularly distraught because it meant he no longer had any excuse to keep his ten foot dingy. Fortunately they soon came around to the idea.

While Mum was a bit perplexed at my decision to join the boys in blue, Dad was not in the least surprised; he claimed to have seen it coming for years. I had, he said in wistful tones, an over-developed sense of honesty and fair play.

Dad worked on the wharf and used to bring home 'gifts' from the various ships he'd been working on. I'd suspected for some time that these presents weren't entirely due to the generosity of the shipowners and I refused to have anything to do with his ill-gotten gains.

My taking the moral high ground annoyed the hell out of Dad. Thinking back, perhaps I did overreact. It wasn't as if he arrived home with a ship's boiler in his duffle-bag, just the odd Taiwanese pocket-knife and Korean home hair-cutting set. Not exactly premium items, though Dad's liquor cabinet was always extremely impressive and often contained brands of alcohol that weren't readily available in New Zealand.

The booze was the most useful of Dad's acquisitions. I have painful memories of some of the other items, particularly the home hair-cutting set. Dad was especially pleased with it. He claimed we'd never have to spend another cent at the hairdressers and was mad keen to try it out. I was 10 years old at the time and my hair was quite long. My father saw this as a great opportunity to try out the kit. I was placed on a stool as Dad got out towels and a broom to give our living room an authentic barber-shop feel. I protested wildly but to no avail: My father had made up his mind.

The implements in the kit looked like something out of a torturer's briefcase. He removed a pair of scissors similar in appearance to pinking shears and began lopping off my hair. Then out came a nasty, buzzing, pair of clippers to do the 'styling'.

After a few minutes of abject fear I calmed down as, astoundingly, he seemed to be doing quite a good job. He was just finishing the hair cut when my grandfather came in and inquired about the technical specifications of the kit. Dad became effusive with his explanations and began waving his arms around in an animated fashion, completely forgetting that he and the clippers were still attached to the back of my head. The result was a large patch of hair was sheared out of my scalp.

'Ooops,' said Dad.

I couldn't see the damage for myself but I knew by the way my grandfather was laughing that it wasn't going to be pretty.

Oh yes, everyone who still had hair was finding it hugely amusing.

My father got a mirror and showed me the carnage. It looked as if a large beast had come along and taken a bite out of my hair. I was devastated and protested to Mum (who was at least making an effort to be sympathetic) that I wouldn't be able to leave the house until it grew back.

'Rubbish,' muttered Dad. 'I'll fix it so no-one will notice.'

Dad's 'fixing' involved him getting a tin of black boot polish and rubbing the sticky, foul smelling paste over the newly whitened piece of my scalp.

'There,' he said, surveying his handiwork. 'Good as new.'

I looked in the mirror. The boot polish didn't look anything like hair. It looked like boot polish. But no matter how much I protested I was told it looked fine, and my head was given a good shine before I was sent off to school the following day.

Of course, this is the sort of occurrence that 10-year-old school boys live for and I was teased unmercifully until my hair grew back.

Much to his disappointment, I never let my father cut my hair again, although he did have the nerve to suggest he get the kit out of storage and give me a quick trim before I became a policeman.

When they came around to the idea of having a member of the constabulary in the family, my parents supported my decision 100 percent.

So now it was down to me: all I had to do was join up. This didn't turn out to be as easy as I'd expected. I don't know why, but I thought I could simply phone the local cop shop and they'd say, 'Ahh Mr Wood, we've been waiting for your call. Pop in and we'll fit you up with a uniform.'

Not the case.

Apparently if I wanted to join the police force there was a fitness test to pass, plus a written examination and an interview. I was also informed that I would not be applying to join the police force but would instead be attempting to become a member of The

New Zealand Police. The word 'force' had recently been dropped as it had been deemed inappropriate for the good citizens of New Zealand to believe that our hardened criminals were being detained by anything other than gentle persuasion. Put straight on that fact, I sent in my application and was began filling out a seemingly unending series of forms.

I soon discovered I was not the only pupil at New Plymouth Boys' High School who wanted to join up. The other (extremely surprising) applicant was a classmate whose nickname was 'Goose'. The reason I found Goose an unlikely candidate was because of his strong Rastafarian leanings. He had embraced the culture with both hands, which was quite unusual for a white, middle-class kid, with straight fair hair. But he played the music, spouted the dogma, wore the T-shirt and actively supported the legalisation of cannabis. Not, one would have thought, a natural choice for the police. However, he was bright, funny, honest and very fit, so, as long as he didn't walk into the interview smoking a joint, I thought he stood a good chance of getting in.

I, on the other hand was struggling. I wasn't worried about the written exam or the interview but I was concerned about my fitness. I wasn't unfit, I was damaged. I'd spent most of my teenage years carrying some injury or other. I was accident prone (and still am) - or at least that's my excuse.

Dad had another theory: he said I was just big and dumb. Reluctantly, I have to admit he had a point. I did charge into things without a great deal of thought and had trouble grasping the fact that,

8

if something doesn't fit where you want it to go, then bashing it till it breaks is probably not going to improve its chances.

My propensity for breaking things also earned me a nickname. I was called Gonzo after the blue fluffy Muppet with the large beak that is always blowing things up. A series of unfortunate incidents at school and the fact that I have a healthy-sized nose ensured the nickname stuck.

So far that year my 'rip, shit or bust' approach to life had resulted in several sprained ankles, a torn calf muscle, cracked ribs, a broken nose and a dislocated shoulder. And it was only March.

Obviously this made taking the police physical exam something of a challenge and after my second postponement my parents began to worry. Sport was put on hold and Mum started keeping close tabs on my activities, the last thing any self-respecting 17-year-old wants.

I had the situation under control until two weeks before my third attempt at the fitness assessment. I was fit, uninjured and confident I could do the required number of push-ups, sit-ups and pull-ups in the stipulated time. And then a friend asked if I wanted to go trail bike riding. Of course I did and I quickly brushed aside everyone's concerns. I knew best and would continue to do so despite overwhelming evidence to the contrary.

So off we went, me on my trusty Kawasaki 100 trail-bike (okay, if you want to get technical, it was Dad's) and my friend on his 'specially designed for the professional circuit' super-bike. I puddled happily around on the Kawi for a while, falling over in the mud a few times but doing no serious damage. Then came the fateful words. 'Do you want a go on my bike?' my mate enquired, overflowing with the generosity of spirit that occurs when you know you have a vastly superior toy.

There was no question of me refusing. This would have been the equivalent of turning up at school wearing women's clothing.

I hopped on, supremely confident that if my friend could handle the bike then it would pose no problems for me. I'd have been alright too if it hadn't been for the power band - a cunning little device that gives you a burst of extra speed when you least expect it. Needless to say the Kawasaki didn't have a power band; the closest it got was a following wind on a steep hill.

The super bike however had an excellent one and it kicked in just as I was attempting a jump I'd eyed up earlier, but had been afraid to tackle on the Kawi. Half way through the jump the bike suddenly took off, shooting from underneath me and leaving me with no option but to fall down.

The 'plummeting through the air' bit wasn't so bad; nor was the 'rolling down the hill and hitting the fence' bit. No, the really painful part occurred when the bike landed on top of me, burning me with its exhaust pipe. Fortunately my friend was quickly on hand to make sure his bike was okay. Once he'd established that my burnt flesh hadn't done too much damage to its paintwork, he picked me up and told me he thought I'd be better off sticking to the Kawasaki. I thought I'd be better off being rushed to Accident and Emergency, but in the end settled for a quiet sit-down with my leg in a nearby stream.

The burn was only superficial but there was some tissue damage and it was bloody sore. I could have postponed the fitness test again but that would have meant missing the next year's intake of police cadets and, much worse, another year at school. Oh, the humanity.

There was nothing for it, Mum bandaged my leg and I sat the fitness test two weeks later. I had no trouble with the push ups, pull ups or sit ups but the run was another story. Completing 2.5 kilometres in14 minutes was hard enough for me fully fit but near impossible with an injured leg.

I can't remember much of the run but I do recall vomiting as I crossed the finish line, which impressed the fitness instructor so much that he overlooked the few seconds I was shy of the time.

I'd already passed the written exam so now I faced the last hurdle, an interview with the district commander.

Goose was in a similar situation, having flown through his fitness exam, but he was extremely nervous about his upcoming interview. I think it was worse for him because of the sacrifice he'd recently made for his chosen career. He had given up the one aspect of his Rastafarian lifestyle that the law took a dim view of. Instead of lighting up, he was relying on a constant diet of Bob Marley music to see him through. It seemed to work but it nearly drove the rest of us insane. Even now I can't hear 'No woman, no cry' without wanting to throttle someone.

My strategy for getting through the interview was a lot less complicated. The only sacrifice I was going to make was to wear a suit and tie. I would also rely on manufactured enthusiasm and keeping my mouth shut (hopefully to prevent career ending utterances from leaking out). The ability to say very little and talk in a stilted and barely comprehensible manner was surely a prerequisite for the police. I made this observation based on watching members of the constabulary interviewed on the news. Not one of them spoke like other members of the human race. It was as if they had become part of this big blue machine that would mutter only carefully guarded words in between awkward silences. I used to imagine the conversations policemen had with their wives.

WIFE: 'Hello dear, did you have a nice day?'

POLICE HUSBAND: (long pause) 'I'm not at liberty to answer that question.'

I learnt later that this manner of speech is secretly implanted into the voice-boxes of all policemen and activated whenever a television camera or microphone comes close.

I practiced the art of appearing enthusiastic while not saying much for several weeks before the interview and become quite good at it. Remaining virtually mute was easy; after all I was a teenager. Enthusiasm was a little harder to come by as I'd been working on being morose and disaffected for several years.

The day of the interview finally arrived and, after Mum had spent several hours making sure I looked respectable, I set off for the station (the police station, that is, not the railway station, which with

12

the benefit of hindsight, would have been a better option). I was wearing the only suit I owned, a black jacket and pants that had only ever been worn to funerals, but had splashed out on a brand new dark blue tie for the occasion.

I arrived early and had to wait for about half an hour. The time went slowly and I remember waiting with a mixture of fear and excitement. As I sat in the station I realised I wanted to join the police more than anything else in the world. The selection process had whet my appetite for the job and I couldn't wait to get started. Watching the day shift cops go about their business only heightened that desire. The station was not particularly busy although there was still plenty going on. Behind the front desk was an older cop and he was handing out advice and forms to an almost constant flow of people, all vying for his attention. He was polite and professional and handled the multitude of problems being placed before him with ease. He wasn't doing anything exceptional but exuded the sort of relaxed confidence that made you feel he was completely in control of the situation. It was the sort of attitude I'd always associated with the police and, as I sat there nervous and excited, I felt in some small way part of it. But I wasn't there yet and would never be if I didn't impress the hell out of the district commander.

Finally my name was called.

I was given directions to the boss's office and told he was ready to see me. I did a final hand pat check to make sure my tie was straight and my fly was done up then headed off. The walk there was almost incident free, except, just before his door, I was

13

caught by the mother of all sneezes. It was one of those sneezes that come from nowhere and strikes with the ferocity of a tropical cyclone before you can get your hankie out. It was also a wet and phlegmy one and I needed to give my hands a good wipe on my handkerchief before meeting the district commander. It would have been poor form to shake hands with sticky digits. I considered stopping in the bathroom to wash my hands but didn't want to keep the top man waiting, so in I went.

The district commander was a nice, old-school cop, with a firm handshake and a relaxed manner. He put me at ease and before long we were chatting about my reasons for wanting to join the police. I'd expected this to come up and had my reply well prepared. My answer contained a healthy mixture of youthful enthusiasm and pro police idealism, with a dollop of community spiritedness thrown in for good measure. I was sure he was impressed but noticed his eyes wandering down to my chest then darting back up again. Aside from the askew glances, it seemed to be going well and we chatted for about an hour.

Towards the end of the interview he touched on the subject of the police's dress code and seemed to spend an unnecessarily long time emphasising how important it was. The DC said that uniforms gave the police respect in the eyes of the public. He reiterated the need for good personal hygiene and reminded me that police officers must keep their uniform in tip top condition at all times, especially the tie. I assured him of my unerring dedication to good grooming (a lie) and he seemed happy.

As the interview ended I grasped his hand firmly and looked him straight in the eye. He returned my gaze and took the opportunity for one final sneaky peek at my chest before giving a little laugh and leading me out of his office. This unnerved me but overall I came away from the interview feeling it had gone well.

Nature and nervous energy caught up with me and I sped to the bathroom to relieve myself. After washing my hands I checked my reflection in the mirror. What I saw stopped me in my tracks. Smack bang in the middle of my tie was the biggest, greenest, lump of phlegm I'd ever seen in my life. Obviously it had deflected off my cupped hands during my pre interview sneeze. I was mortified. I'd just spent an hour chatting to the man who held my career prospects in his hands with a huge, wobbly, mountain of gunk sticking out of my chest. It looked like a less savoury version of the thing that burst from John Hurt's stomach in the movie "Alien".

Suddenly the district commander's concerns about my personal hygiene made sense. I mean, how would it look to have constables out there pounding the beat covered in snot? I couldn't believe it; a dollop of lung butter had blown my chance of selection. It was so unfair. I wanted to rip my tie off and run into the boss's office pleading that it wasn't my fault and that actually it was part of the tie's design - the latest in wearable body fluid from Hugo Boss - but instead I cleaned my tie, shoved it in my pocket, and skulked home.

I didn't tell Mum or Dad about the incident - no point worrying them and I wasn't sure how much damage had been done.

Still, I think they worked out that things hadn't gone to plan when I started swotting my old biology books and told Dad not to sell the dingy.

THE DEMON ALCOHOL: PART ONE

By now you'd have thought I'd done everything possible to screw up my chances of getting into the police, but I wasn't finished yet, oh no.

My next attempt at career suicide came as I waited, somewhat dejectedly, for the results of my application. My parents were going away for the weekend and my sister was also away. This left me alone in the house.

Mum and Dad agonised over this prospect for weeks - not because they didn't trust me (the fools), but because they had bought a new television and my track record of breaking things made them fear for its safety. In fact, the only instructions they gave me before going were: 'Stay away from the liquor cabinet and don't blow up the television.' Not unreasonable requests and I assured them they had no cause for concern. Sadly I was wrong.

Everything would have been fine were it not for Geoff Redfern, a good friend from school whose ambition in life was not to join the police. Geoff didn't have criminal leanings but he did have a rather liberal attitude to rules. This had got us into trouble before - nothing serious, but from a parental perspective, Geoff definitely fell into the category of a bad influence.

From my point of view he was a cool guy who was heaps of fun and exactly the sort of chap you'd invite round, if you found yourself alone in the house. Naturally, once you'd invited Geoff you also had to invite Quentin, another of my friends, who had the uncanny ability of being a really bad influence without seeming to be. He was one of those guys that your parents think is the sensible one. How often I'd heard the words, 'You can go if Quentin's going; he won't let you do anything stupid.' They were right; he wouldn't let me do anything stupid: he'd do it, and I'd get the blame. Still, he was my best mate and he normally brought the beer.

So, there we were, alone in the house with lots of alcohol and no parental supervision. We had everything we needed for a great night, but something was missing. Girls.

Tragically all three of us were without girlfriends and it was the cause of great concern. After all, we were young, handsome (in the right light), fitish, and technically sane men. What woman in her right mind wouldn't want to go out with us? Almost the entire female population of New Plymouth appeared to be the answer. What was wrong with them? How could they not see how funny Quentin's impersonation of the forward pack of the New Plymouth Boys' High School rugby First XV was? We were confused. We had so much to offer and there were so few takers.

The night got later, the beer stack grew smaller, and our eligibility increased. Then, just as we reached the zenith of our irresistibility, Geoff came up with a plan. It was a great plan. And like all world-beating ideas it was brilliant in its simplicity. All we had to do was drink more alcohol then go for a walk, where we would find the streets lined with women who would instantly recognise our, oh so obvious, charms.

This was the kind of thinking Geoff was famous for.

Quentin was quick to spot a flaw. We were out of beer.

We sat and pondered the problem and when it looked like there was no solution, Quentin decided to go home. This turned out to be one of the finest decisions he has ever made, because just after he left, Geoff came up with another plan. It involved Dad's liquor cabinet.

A little voice whispered in my ear, 'Don't blow up the television set and don't touch the liquor cabinet.'

Isn't it funny how the memory plays tricks on you? That evening I could swear Dad's instructions had finished with the phrase 'but it's up to you son.' Besides, the television was undamaged and a 50 per cent pass is acceptable in most tests.

Now that I'd nullified that concern we decided it was safe to hook into Dad's whisky, rum, vodka and most fatally, saki, (a present from one of those generous shipping lines).

Once Geoff and I agreed that we had consumed the required amount of alcohol (there was none left), we set out into the night, in search of... something. We'd forgotten the first plan by now and were winging it. We decided that it must have been a burger as the munchies were setting in. A combination of the cold night air and the nasty mixture of drinks we'd consumed seemed to exacerbate our drunkenness and make everything seem extremely funny. We wesaved down the street, laughing at the hilarious footpath and giggling at the incredibly amusing other footpath. Once the pavement had run out of jokes we set off to find a new source of fun. This came in the form of a large fence outside New Plymouth Girls High School. The fence had obviously been constructed so that drunken people could climb up it and sing to the girls in the dormitories. So this is what we did, completely forgetting that it was the school holidays and the only people we were likely to rouse were the cleaning staff. Even if we'd remembered we were too far gone to care, and it was only when the top bar of the fence broke and sent us toppling to the ground, that our tuneless serenade ended.

I thought Geoff's fall had been particularly good so I pulled a large stalk of grass out of the ground and gave it to him as the "Brave Man Award".

He was touched and accepted the award proudly. After a moving speech in which he thanked his mother, his agent, his motorbike, a lamp post and the person on the other side of the road, he set off to share the award with his adoring public. He did this by staggering drunkenly into the middle of the road waving the stalk of grass wildly above his head. Eventually the fact that he was in immediate danger of being squashed like a bug eked its way into Geoff's booze-soaked brain and he joined me back on the footpath.

Then we remembered the reason we were out - hamburgers. The search for true love had well and truly been surpassed by the need for food.

We headed towards town.

On the way we passed the Devon Motor Lodge. At first glance you wouldn't think there was anything remarkable about this establishment. It was a perfectly respectable Motor Lodge, with a perfectly respectable motor (presumably) and perfectly respectable lodgings. But it did have one thing that set it apart from the rest of the street - a fountain. Quite an impressive fountain too. With three tiers. The bottom level featured a big round pool which was decorated with pottery fishes that squirted streams of water out of their mouths. The second tier was made up of the metal wings and harp of a flying angel. The top tier was the head of the angel and I'm pretty sure she wore a beautiful crown with water squirting from each of its prongs.

I must pause at this point to apologise to anyone who has seen the Devon Motor Lodge fountain, for any inaccuracies in this description. I'm quite old and I've taken quite a few blows to the head. I wouldn't be surprised to find out that the Devon Motor Lodge hasn't even got a fountain. All I know is that we were in the presence of a large wet fountainy thing and it was somewhere in the vicinity of the Devon Motor Lodge. Anyway, for the purposes of this story let's just believe everything I say.

As any intoxicated person knows, it is physically impossible to go past a fountain without jumping into it. So in we leapt for a jolly fine frolic. I was quite happy splashing around with the fishes at the bottom but Geoff wanted to plant the Brave Man Award in the angel's crown. This had a lovely poetic feel to it so I gave him a leg up to the third tier. He scrambled to the top and sat down happily trying to insert the stalk of grass into one of the water pipes. I was just about to go up and help him when a flashing blue light caught

21

my eye. I turned around to see several police cars and a dog van zooming past us on the other side of the road.

'I wonder who they're after?' called Geoff from the top of the fountain.

'I dunno,' I replied, hopping out to investigate.

I watched as the police cars disappeared down a dip in the road about 500 metres from where I was standing. A dripping wet Geoff joined me at the edge of the footpath.

'Where've they gone?' he asked.

It was a bloody good question. They'd gone into the dip but hadn't appeared at the other side of the hill. I got a very bad feeling about this. A feeling that intensified when I looked behind me at the fountain. The crown was badly misshapen and water was squirting everywhere. A couple of the fish I'd been chatting to weren't looking that healthy either.

'It's alright, here they are.' yelled Geoff as the patrol cars roared up the road towards us.

As the first car screeched to a stop it dawned on me that we may be in a bit of trouble. It was a weird feeling because we didn't think we were doing anything wrong. As far as we were concerned we were spreading joy and love everywhere we went. We certainly hadn't meant to upset anyone or damage anything. However, I had the presence of mind to realise that explaining this to the police officer who was leaping out of his car might be a bit tricky, so I decided to take the only option left to me - I was going to run like hell.

I suggested loudly to Geoff that he do the same and then legged it.

I didn't stop to see what my mate was doing, I just sprinted as fast as I could down the side of a nearby house. I carried on through someone's back yard and then leapt over a fence. There was a lot of noise behind me and I knew the cops were chasing me. I was operating on survival instinct now and just kept running - through another back yard, down the side of another house, across a side street and into an alleyway. It was dark and I was terrified but I was so pumped full of adrenalin that nothing was going to stop me. I knew that if I got caught it would be the end of my police career and I reasoned that if Geoff and I both escaped the authorities might not be able to identify us. Geoff was quite nippy and I thought there was a good chance of us eluding capture.

I heard a dog bark behind me and I raced out of the alley and into the yard of another house. I was running as fast as I could and just as I'd reached full stretch someone grabbed me around the neck and threw me to the ground. I lay there stunned, gasping for breath and looking wildly around for whomever it was that had dropped me. I expected a policeman to jump on me and slap handcuffs on my wrists but nothing happened. There was no-one in sight. I got up cautiously and realised what had happened. Stretched between the side of the house and the fence was a long plastic rope. I'd been apprehended by a clothes line.

I rubbed my neck, it was sore but there didn't appear to be any permanent damage. Thinking back I was lucky I didn't break it (my neck, not the clothesline).

The fall brought about a change of tactics. Instead of running like hell I decided to sneak quietly off into the night. My initial burst of speed had put some distance between myself and my pursuers but I could hear them searching the houses behind me and lights were going on all over the place, including in the house I was standing beside. I had no idea where I was but I wanted to get away from the houses so I snuck across the road into a field. Creeping along the tree line and moving very slowly, I kept going until I could no longer hear the commotion behind me. Finally I climbed over a fence into what I thought was another field. It wasn't, it was a grave yard. This seemed appropriate because if I got caught then my police career was dead.

I sat on a gravestone and felt miserable. I was afraid to stay where I was but equally feared going home in case the police were waiting for me. I was also scared of what Mum and Dad were going to say. They were due home at lunchtime the next day and suddenly my faith in their being reasonable about the depletion of the liquor cabinet had evaporated. What started as a misdemeanour had quickly become a capital offence. I was also beginning to worry about Geoff - maybe he wasn't as quick as I thought.

I stayed where I was for about three hours until the risk of piles and the approaching morning forced me to move. It was a long, lonely, trudge home, however I cheered up a bit when I turned into our street and saw that it hadn't been cordoned off and there weren't any police cars outside our house. I rushed inside, expecting to see

Geoff there. Then we'd have a good laugh and tell fantastic stories of our miraculous escapes.

The house was deserted. All that remained were empty bottles and the sickly stench of spilt booze and poor decisions. I flopped hopelessly into the lounge chair and tried to figure out my next move. I couldn't ring Geoff's parents. It was still very early in the morning and he was supposed to be spending the night with me. Besides, he could still have been hiding somewhere. To alert anyone now would sink us for sure. I toyed with the idea of ringing Quentin's place in the vain hope that Geoff may have gone there but didn't want to risk waking his parents. In the end I decided to go to bed and hope for the best. I've used this ploy many times in my life and can safely say it has never worked. It was spectacularly unsuccessful on this occasion as I was woken a couple of hours later by the phone.

I stumbled out of bed just as the hang-over from hell made an appearance. The sun tried to burn its way through my skull and the phone's piercing ring sent severe jolts through every nerve in my body. I answered the call. It was Geoff's dad. He wanted to speak to my father. This was not a good sign. I explained that I was the only one home and I wondered if I could help. I was informed that I'd done more than enough already. I guessed that Geoff must have turned up somewhat worse for wear (I'm extremely intuitive) and asked if I could speak with him. I was curtly informed that I was never to contact him again. The sinking feeling in my stomach had now reached the lower strata of the earth's crust and was contemplating a mission to the seventh level of Hades.

Fortunately, Mrs Redfern, who must have been standing near the phone, urged her husband to take pity on me. He yielded grudgingly and let me speak to Geoff.

The person who came on the phone was a far cry from the 'devil may care', fun loving rebel I had been with the night before. This new Geoff Redfern was promising never to drink again and proclaiming to have given up his evil ways. Only after several minutes of regret and remorse, which I assume were for his parent's sake, did I finally find out what had happened.

Geoff had come to the conclusion that fleeing was the best option seconds after I had. Unfortunately, in his saki-addled state, he had been less accurate than me in selecting an escape route. He turned around and ran smack bang into the side of the dog van, then fell semi-conscious onto the footpath. From there the police simply picked him up and threw him in the back of a patrol car. Possibly their easiest arrest ever. On the drive back to the station he said the cops kept asking who his mate was. My stomach heaved and I felt sick. Then Geoff perked up as he proudly informed me that he hadn't dobbed me in and had told the police he was alone.

A glimmer of hope.

'So they don't know who I am then?' I asked optimistically.

'Well I didn't tell them,' he replied, 'Unfortunately, when dad arrived at the station he said 'Was Glenn Wood with him?'

The glimmer died. That was it; I'd been fingered by Geoff's old man. I was history. I might as well pack the striped toothpaste because I was on my way to the big house to spend the rest of my days with a large room mate who wasn't too particular where he placed his penis. Forget the New Zealand Police: I was about to become employed by the chain gang.

Geoff finished by saying he had gained the impression that the police were a bit upset and wanted a word with me. I replaced the receiver and went into the bathroom for a panic vomit then crawled into bed and pulled the covers over my head.

For the next few hours I weighed up the pros and cons of running away and becoming a peasant farmer in Chad. In the end I decided that looking pathetic and pleading stupidity was probably a better option.

My first obstacle would be Mum and Dad and I put off phoning the police until I'd fessed up to them. They weren't due home for another couple of hours and the time moved as slowly as a snail with a groin injury. Finally I heard the car in the driveway. I was sick with nervousness and, I suspect, a minor case of saki poisoning.

As soon as Mum saw me she knew something was wrong. Mothers are good like that: they have an uncanny knack of spotting a carefully constructed and sanitised story before you can even open your mouth. She cut to the chase.

'What have you done to the television?'

I told them the TV was fine but they should expect a visit from the police shortly and that I'd probably be spending the rest of my life eating liver and maggot stew and making number plates.

Mum looked relieved about the television.

The thing they were most angry about was that I had disobeyed a strict instruction. There were protracted discussions about loss of trust and ruined lives but they eventually calmed down and tried to work out if anything could be salvaged from the mess I'd created. Dad said the first thing I should do was to ring the police and confess. I was also to make a suitably humble apology to Geoff's parents.

The police were surprisingly relaxed when I phoned them. To me this was life or death stuff - my whole future hung in the balance - but to them it was just another drunk and disorderly. I was informed that they had my details and a detective would be around to see me the following Tuesday night.

I was secretly pleased about that: a detective, wow. I guess if you are going to stuff things up you might as well do it big time.

Dad set the wharfie network into action and had a chat with a few of his police mates to see how much damage I had done. The general consensus was that as I hadn't actually been arrested, it would be up to the detective in charge of the case as to what action, if any, was taken. Those two words "if any" gave me a sliver of hope which I clutched onto with both hands. Everything that had happened had inflamed my desire to join the police. I hadn't enjoyed being pursued but it made me think how cool it would be to be the ones doing the chasing.

Tuesday evening rolled around with the speed of that snail with the groin injury, who had now pulled a muscle in his lower back and was on accident compensation. All day I'd practiced being humble and remorseful and had it down pat. Mum did her bit as well and bought some nice biscuits for the detective. By the time the he arrived we were the picture of a good, honest, hard working, family. My sister (a bit of a tomboy) was even wearing a dress.

The detective was a young guy who treated the situation with the right balance of gravity and humour. He started by impressing on me the potentially disastrous situation I had placed myself in. However, it was felt that I had played the lesser role in the activities of the night. I thought this was a bit unfair on Geoff but a look from Dad told me this wasn't the time to argue.

Apparently the initial complaint was laid by a driver who was convinced that Geoff was trying to hit his car with a bit of wood. I explained that my friend's only weapon had been a blade of grass and that he was just waving it in the air. My explanation was accepted but I was told that as a complaint had been laid and because there was property damage involved (the fountain); charges would have to be made. I held my breath as he finished the sentence. The prosecution was being brought against Geoff.

I was relieved and horrified at the same time. I said that neither of us had set out to hurt anyone or damage anything. The detective realised this and told me not to worry. Geoff was being bought up on a minor drunk and disorderly offence and would probably just get a small fine and a few hours community service. He said if they had believed the damage had been intentional then the charges would have been much more serious. He added that I was extremely lucky not to have been apprehended on the night because I would have been arrested and court proceedings put in motion. As it was, he now had the power of discretion and after discussing it with his colleagues he had decided to let me off with a warning.

It was all I could do to keep from hugging him. I felt like the large boulder that had been crushing the life out of me for the last few days had just rolled off.

Having finished telling me off the detective relaxed back in his chair, took a biscuit (pleasing my mother) and said, "So you want to join the Police eh."

He then spent the next hour telling me what a great job it was and how he'd had a look at my results and the general feeling around the station was that I had a very good chance of getting in. He said the top brass was prepared to look on this incident as youthful exuberance and as long as a lesson was learnt then no harm was done. He gave a long smile and I'm sure he winked at my father.

'Actually,' he said 'we've decided that anyone who can outrun two cops and a dog is better off on our side of the law.'

I was astounded. Far from blowing my chances it seemed I'd enhanced them. The net effect of this conversation was that I now considered police officers to be the coolest guys and gals on the planet and was prepared to work my butt off to join them. The detective gave me firm handshake and a reminder to stay out of trouble as he left. The warning was quite unnecessary because I planned to shut myself in my room and study for the rest of the year. Well, for a couple of weeks anyway.

Naturally my parents were thrilled, though I was left in no doubt that my disobedience hadn't been forgotten and a lot of work was required to fill the hole I'd dug myself.

And of course there was Geoff, who had copped an unfair amount of the blame. He went to court the following Monday and, after pleading guilty to a drunk and disorderly charge, was given a smack on the wrist and 20 hours community service, which he spent playing table tennis at an old folks home.

Geoff's parents didn't stay mad with me for long but the incident didn't endear him to my parents who were still somewhat blinkered when it came to recognising my ability to get into trouble without assistance. The most galling part of the whole incident was that once again Quentin came out of it smelling of roses. It was well known he'd been with us for the first part of the evening but had shown the good sense to leave before things got out of hand. Good sense my arse! It was just pure dumb luck that he wasn't with us when we discovered the saki. Geoff and I knew that if he'd stuck around for another five minutes then he'd have been first up the fountain and into the Police van, but as usual he'd dodged the bullet.

My letter of acceptance into the New Zealand Police came several weeks later. I was one of 78 Cadets who had been selected from over 350 applicants. Goose received his letter of acceptance on the same day and we were both to become part of the 24th General Poananga Cadet Wing, beginning training on the 22nd of January 1980. I had just turned eighteen.

THE BOOK

The last thing I did before leaving for Trentham was fall in love. It was inevitable really. I'd been involved with several girls over the past few years but had been unable to find anyone I could connect with (metaphorically speaking of course).

I met this girl the week before I left New Plymouth.

Quentin and I had been camp counsellors at a YMCA camp over the summer. Not through any Christian need to help the youth in our community but because female counsellors also worked there and we thought it would be a good way to meet girls. It turned out that quite a few of the girls had joined up just to meet boys, so everyone was happy.

Anyway, we were having a farewell bash at the Devon Motor Lodge (heavy irony) before I left town and the camp leaders from all the different YMCA camps were there, including some I hadn't met before.

The girl who caught my eye was called Carey and she was a leader for the young explorers troop. I was young and quite fancied exploring her, so I got a friend to introduce us and we hit it off extremely well. She admitted having seen me riding my motorbike past Girls High on my way to school and I admitted that Girls High wasn't actually on my way to school.

I soon discovered that she was leaving New Plymouth as well. She was going to Palmerston North to attend teacher's training college. This was good news as I already had several friends in Palmerston North and it gave me an excuse to visit her on any free weekends I had.

Later that night we both professed our undying love for each other (based on several hours of snogging) and promised to write and visit whenever possible.

So the next week, love sick, car sick and hung over, I prepared to bid New Plymouth and Carey a fond farewell and set sail for pastures new. Except I wouldn't actually be sailing, I'd be spending eight hours on a smelly old bus, sitting next to Goose and listening to Bob Marley music.

Still, it was the end of an era, my childhood and young adulthood were over and I was about to enter a new, more sober time, where I would prove my worth through hard work, restraint and self denial. Possibly.

My parents and friends waved me off at the bus stop. My friends looked sad, my parents looked relieved.

Goose and I confirmed on the bus trip that we had very little in common besides the police and rugby. Despite this we got along well and it was a relief to discover he was as nervous as I about our new career. We both found it difficult to explain why we had joined up.

There is an old Police saying which states that the real reason for being a police officer is because you want to be one. This mind numbingly obvious statement is actually quite an insightful one. If you don't look too closely it is a very appealing job for a young guy.

Fancy threads, fast cars, guns, fighting bad guys, status and power. All this and they pay you as well! What could be better?

It had never occurred to me that all this came at a price. I knew how badly I had misjudged the situation when I got my first glimpse of the Trentham police training college. It was like a scene from an old war movie: Colditz minus the searchlights and guard towers. This turned out to be an apt description as the official classification of the police training facilities at Trentham was 'First World War Barracks' and the title of our leader was 'The Commandant'.

In fact, let me quote directly from The Commandant's Message in my police year book. 'Most of the memories [of Trentham] will revolve around the decay, the austerity and the bleakness of Trentham on a rainy day.' The only surprise was that it didn't end with the words – 'Welcome to Hell'.

Our barracks were long, cold, wooden huts with rusty corrugated iron walls, no insulation, bad plumbing and hard plank beds. This was in the years before sleeping on wooden slats became popular, courtesy of the clever marketing of the futon. I take my hat off to anyone who can convince people that lying on planks is comfortable and good for you. My experience was completely the opposite.

The cadet barracks sat side by side in a large concrete and gravel compound. We were to occupy two of the huts. The rest were filled with recruits (older police trainees or 'Gumbies' as we called them, for reasons I have never been able to work out), Ministry of

Transport trainees (snakes), our instructors (sir, madam or God), our classrooms, the sick bay and the mess hall.

Whoever designed the compound must have had a great sense of humour because our sterile, barn like, miserable, grotty barracks were surrounded by cute, white picket fences. The type of fences that doomed prostitutes in bad movies dream of having around their country cottages, just before they are blown away by their pimps. Only Hollywood or the New Zealand police could come up with juxtaposition like that.

Our neighbours were the army (who we rarely saw because they were too busy killing things) and the CIT which was a training institute for postal workers, the majority of whom were female. As there were no females in our wing (women were only allowed to join as recruits, I'm not sure why) this was a much-visited institution and many of the cadets came to be on first-name terms with the security guards who were hired to keep us out.

Once we'd had a chance to have a look around and convince ourselves that perhaps it wasn't as bad as it appeared, we were called into the camp hall to meet our instructors and the other cadets.

The instructors' jobs was to convince us that, yes, it was as bad as it appeared. The first thing they told us was that we had the honour of being the last wing to go through Trentham, as the barracks were scheduled for demolition and a brand new (luxury) college was being built in Porirua. Lucky, lucky us. As we knew no better, even this sadistic snippet of information didn't dampen our spirits. Because basically we were too young and stupid to realise what we'd got ourselves into.

Once the instructors had introduced themselves we were told that we'd be given our room numbers and course instructions in alphabetical order.

I hated that. Being called Wood meant I was always one of the last to find out what was going on. I muttered about this to the guy next to me and instantly found a soul mate. His name was Phil Wooding and he was the only cadet further down the alphabetical ladder than I was. We instantly declared a loathing for all people with the surname Anderson and sat impatiently waiting our turn.

Eventually we found out our room numbers and sped off to see who we were going to share our lives with for the next year. This factor had a large bearing on how much you enjoyed your time at Trentham. There were two cadets in every room and you were separated by only about three metres of wooden floor. It was a bit like prison in some respects. If you got the big smelly psycho killer who wanted to be your 'special friend,' then your stay wouldn't be a pleasant one.

Fortunately my room-mate was okay. He was an even tempered, quiet guy called Rob who laughed at my jokes. I liked him instantly.

Phil wasn't so lucky; his room-mate's only outstanding feature was that he had no elbows. He also had overactive sweat glands. The guy produced more salt than Siberia. Not an attractive quality in a room-mate.

However, things could have been worse. Smelly and annoying

as Phil's room- mate was, at least he didn't have any major psychological problems. A cadet just up the hall from us had a room-mate who was a right nutter. The first sign that a cuckoo had escaped from the clock came when the room-mate began walking up and down the hallway making sounds like a motor car, complete with the occasional missed gear change.

Rumour had it that eventually some of the instructors noticed this particular cadet was one truncheon short of a riot squad and sent him in for psychological evaluation. He failed. Unfortunately, not before he had pulled a knife on his room-mate. When the incident was reported, the loony was then whisked away by the chief inspector and was immediately promoted to district commander. Just kidding.

After the knife incident he disappeared, never to be seen at Trentham again, though sometimes, late at night I swear I could hear the sound of a Ferrari being badly driven up and down the hall.

The truly frightening thing about the whole incident was that it had taken a term and a half for our instructors to notice they'd employed a wacko. The police were a bit like that, they were always so concerned with detail that sometimes they would miss the bigger picture.

Phil's room was right next door to mine and, as our beds were only separated by only 10 centimetres of wall, we were able to develop a sophisticated communication system by tapping messages on the wood. Having an early warning code was vital at Trentham. There were a whole host of dangers that required careful negotiation and forewarned was forearmed.

In the first term our instructors took particular pleasure in springing instant inspections on us, often at some ungodly hour in the morning. This meant that at a moment's notice there would be a cry of "Stand by your beds!" and we would be required to do just that as our instructors came through and examined our rooms. An extremely high standard of neatness and organisation was expected of us, which was particularly unfair given that we were all teenage lads alone for the first time without our mums. Our apron strings weren't just cut - they were fed into a threshing machine.

No posters were allowed on the walls and all our belongings had to be stored as per draconian police regulations. Our clothes were to be neatly folded and stored in a chest of drawers that stood beside our beds. The drawer on the right was to contain socks (balled up one inside the other) whilst the drawer on the left contained underpants (ironed and folded as per underwear regulation 54 subsection b). A sock being discovered in the underpants drawer was punishable by decapitation. Punishment was equally harsh for any breaches of the following tidiness proclamations:

- Beds were to contain one under sheet, one over sheet and one blanket. Any other blankets were to be folded (without wrinkles) and placed on top of your wardrobe. The curve of the fold had to face the front of the room and the edge of the blankets had to be flush with the top of the wardrobe.

- Your bed was to be made the instant you left it and hospital corners were mandatory. The sheet had to be folded over the blanket exactly twelve inches from the head of the bed and the fold itself had to be exactly twelve inches long. Our instructors carried rulers with them and measured the folds during inspections.

- Pillows were to be placed above the fold, with the crease of the pillow facing towards the wall. The remainder of the bed had to be completely flat and wrinkle free. (As we were constantly reminded, wrinkles were the enemy of an ordered bed.)

- Uniforms had to be hung up in the wardrobe, shirts on the left and trousers on the right. Only your uniform could hang in the wardrobe and every garment had to be in inspection order. This meant knife edge creases on the sleeves of the shirts and the front of the trousers. If a double line appeared on any garment you were in breach of regulations and were shot at dawn.

- Two pairs of regulation black shoes were to be placed at the bottom of the wardrobe directly under the trousers. The toe of the shoes was not to protrude in front of an imaginary line drawn along the front of the frame of the wardrobe.

- Shoes had to be highly polished (by the rather unsavoury spit method) to such a degree that the inspector must be able to clearly make out his face in the shine on the toe.

- Finally your room had to be clear from dust (a white glove was used to detect any rogue particles) and your windows smear free.

Failure to comply with these and about a billion other anally retentive rules was instantly punished by an instructor requiring you to put your name in "The Book". The Book was a cruel and unusual punishment as it had the potential to rob a cadet of what he prized most: his weekends.

The system was simple and effective. As soon as a cadet accrued three entries on his booking card he was confined to barracks for the weekend. This meant the cadet was only allowed in his room and the gymnasium. He was also required to report to the duty sergeant in full dress uniform every two hours, from 7am til 9pm. If the duty sergeant was having a bad day (which they inevitably were, having drawn weekend duty) he could inspect you, and if your uniform wasn't up to scratch - you guessed it - name in The Book again. Avoiding this repeat booking generally meant spending most of the two hours between inspections ironing your shirts and gobbing on your shoes. It was not a good way to spend your precious time off.

Inspections could occur without warning at any time, day or night, and were particularly harsh during the first term. Often we would be called out of our beds at 5 am and made to form three-bleary eyed ranks outside the barracks as our instructors went through the building like a tornado. We would return to our rooms 10 minutes later to find them trashed. Our drawers would be tipped out, blankets strewn all over the bed, uniforms thrown in a crumpled pile on the floor and shoes tossed around the room. We were then expected to get everything back in tip top shape for our daily inspection at 8am.

Advance notice of these smash and grab raids was very hard to come by but great if you could get it. Which is where the tapping system came in handy. Three rapid taps meant a snap inspection looked imminent. This gave you time to smooth down your bed and hide contraband, such as Penthouse magazines, satanic rock music or liquor. Being caught with said items was risky, if not fatal. A double booking was the least you could expect, with the ultimate punishment, instant dismissal from training, also a possibility. Though, to be fair, dismissal was generally reserved for more heinous crimes, like trying to stab your room-mate or being seen within a 10km radius of the commandant's daughter.

Early warning was also required for protection against the Gumbies. There was an instant animosity between cadets and recruits. The recruits were older than us (normally in their mid-20s) and were at Trentham for a three month crash course. They looked on us as jumped-up kids with ideas above our station, which of course we were. We looked at them as wimpy losers who took the easy course because they weren't good enough to get in as cadets. This was grossly unfair but right from the start we were a big-headed bunch of bastards. We had been told early in the course that we were seen as officer material and naturally, this went straight to our heads.

Thus began the ritual taunting of the Gumbies.

We took particular delight in ambushing new recruits and giving them a damn fine soaking. (Once the Gumbies had been at Trentham for a few weeks they sussed out our tactics, so the best time to hit them was when they were green.) The cadet armoury contained many and various water weapons that were kept in a state of constant readiness.

Our most spectacular success came in the second term when a group of new recruits arrived. Early in the morning of their second day these raw recruits were called out of their barracks by a barking senior sergeant who lined them up outside then abused the crap out of them. The 'senior sergeant' was in fact a very mature looking cadet who had 'borrowed' an officer's uniform from the stores - a highly dangerous feat.

While they stood in nervous and confused rows on the parade ground we struck. A three-pronged attack had been conceived to achieve maximum soakage. Cadet force A appeared from the opposite barracks in front of the Gumbie ranks, all howling at the top of their lungs and armed with high-pressure fire hoses. A second group of cadets attacked from the sides with water balloons and various other watery projectiles. The third section attacked from above, tipping rubbish bins full of water over the recruits from the roofs of their own barracks. The Gumbies scattered in all directions yelling in ineffective anger. Their bellowed threats had little effect; it was hard to feel threatened by a group of soggy guys in wet pyjamas.

Our victory had been complete and devastating. We celebrated with a hearty chorus of "The Gumbie Song", which went something like this:

(Sung to the tune of 'Cindy')

'I wish I was a Gumbie,

A hanging on a tree,

And every time a Senior passed,

He'd take a kick at me.

Get along home Gumbie, Gumbie.

Get along home Gumbie, Gumbie.

Get along home Gumbie, Gumbie.

I'll kick you up the arse.'

Well, we weren't there for our lyrical abilities.

I think our instructors were secretly impressed by the audacity of our attack because our punishment was less severe than expected. We were made to run up to the water tower and back.

The water tower stood at the top of a very steep gravel hill and it really tested your fitness. On this particular occasion, we were still high on the adrenalin rush from the battle and conquered the tower with relative ease. We even had enough breath to belt out another verse of the Gumbie song from the top of the tower, which earned us another lap on our return. This time the only sound at the top was everyone gasping for breath.

The Gumbies had their revenge, however. It came late one night when we were fast asleep. We all slept with our feet facing our wardrobes (as per regulations) and our heads resting on one pillow against the corrugated iron sides of the barracks outer wall. On the night of the recruits revenge we were in for a rude awakening. We were jolted from deep sleep by what sounded like a large herd of horses, wearing tin horseshoes stampeding across an iron lake. It was one of those sounds that starts quietly in your subconscious and builds to a thundering crescendo that bursts into your frontal lobes, causing your brain to leak out your ears (a bit like a 'Spice Girls' song).

The horrendous noise was caused by Gumbies sprinting along the outside of our barracks running a broomstick along the corrugated iron wall, literally inches from our heads. We staggered out of our beds, completely disorientated, as the second wave of recruits ran through the inside of our barracks turning our own fire hoses on us and soaking our beds with water balloons. I'm sure revenge was sweet, especially as we had to explain the state of our rooms to a very unsympathetic group of instructors at inspection the next morning. Put your name in The Book, cadet.

Danger also lurked in our own corridors. A favourite late-night pastime of some cadets was a brutal ritual known as stacking. One moment you'd be lying on your bed, minding your own business, the next your door would burst open and 10 to 12 hulking cadets would leap on top of you, one after another, forming a vertical stack of bodies that weighed about two tons. One of two things happened at this stage, either your ribs or your bed broke.

If an injury happened or damage occurred you were left to explain it yourself. There was an unwritten rule that you never ratted on a fellow cadet (not for anything short of attempted homicide, anyway). A few cadets did complain about being picked on. From that moment their lives became hell as revenge stackings, with even more stackees crushing them, became an almost nightly occurrence.

I was on the receiving end of only one stacking and a most unpleasant experience it was. The breath was squashed out of my lungs and my eyeballs nearly popped out of their sockets. Being a member of the stacking crew was almost as bad as being on the receiving end. I only took part in one. The target was Phil's room-mate and the idea of squashing the annoying sod was too appealing to turn down. I was third in the stack and got caught in the ear by the elbow of the cadet on top of me. It was extremely uncomfortable. Still, we effectively squished the enemy so it wasn't a complete loss. Felt a bit mean afterwards, though.

I was lined up for another stacking several weeks later but thanks to good intelligence from my room-mate I was able to rig up a dummy consisting of some 4x2s, a couple of blankets and a wig. When the stacking occurred I was hiding in my wardrobe and the unfortunate cadet at the bottom of the stack popped a rib on the 4x2. Served him right.

While stacking was undeniably brutal it was seldom malicious. Everyone got done once or twice and as I said earlier it was only ever nasty if you were foolish enough to complain about it.

In general the cadets got on pretty well, mainly because we were all in the same boat. Naturally there were a few personality clashes (some cadets didn't have any) but no more than you'd expect from a large group of highly competitive young males. A certain amount of territory marking went on early in the piece but that soon settled down as we became too knackered to care about anything other than surviving the course.

The instructors fostered our competitive natures by splitting us into three sections according to our surnames. We had A Section (A through F), B Section (G through M) and C Section (N through Z).

A, B and C Sections: the New Zealand Police once again demonstrating all the imagination of boiled cabbage.

Inter-section rivalry was encouraged in almost every aspect of cadet life and a sort of alphabetical apartheid developed. We were constantly played off against one another with a disproportionate degree of importance attached to being in the 'winning' section. I understand why the Police encouraged this attitude. It was to instil in us a sense of loyalty and trust in "our" team, but it could also be destructive and dangerous.

A graphic example occured several months into the course when a friend of mine named Alex was selected as flag bearer for an forthcoming ceremony. I can't remember what the event was but three cadets (one from each section) were chosen to represent the wing. It was quite an honour to have been selected and all three were very proud of their part in the event. Uniforms were pressed to an unprecedented degree, shoes were spit-polished till mouths ran dry, and you could have shaved on the single prominent creases running down the arms of their shirts. As it turned out getting their uniforms up to scratch was the easy bit.

The hard part was the almost endless drill the poor sods had to endure.

I was secretly pleased at having been passed over for selection, even though, to be honest, I was never really in the hunt. My marching and drill abilities were regularly called into question. I tried, God knows I tried, but my innate clumsiness shone through and I often found myself being the only one who was marching in step.

Alex, on the other hand, had almost precognitive drill powers. He could sense an 'eyes right' coming seconds before it happened and he'd have his head whipped around while I was still trying to work out if I was supposed to turn to my right, or theirs. His 'about turn' was a blur and his 'left wheel' a joy to behold. He also worked out long before the rest of us that 'stand at ease' didn't give you carte blanche to let rip with that fart you'd been holding in since the last march past.

Unfortunately it was his exceptional ability on the parade ground that cost him his career in the police.

It was a blisteringly hot day and as usual the three 'chosen ones' were engaged in drill practice. They were required to stand at full attention while a mock raising-of-the-flag ceremony occurred. As usual the police did nothing by halves and trotted out the 'extended mix' ceremony complete with boring, pointless speeches and a lot of strutting about by senior officers who should have known better.

While all this was going on Alex and his mates had to stand

perfectly still, their legs unwavering, arms pinned by their sides, (thumbs along trouser creases, boys) backs straight and heads held high.

Staying in this position for any length of time is bloody difficult, but in 30 degree heat on a solid concrete parade ground, it was nigh on impossible. Alex lasted about twenty minutes before heat exhaustion set in and he collapsed in a dead faint, falling forward onto the parade ground. His head hit the concrete with a sickening crack. His concentration had been so great and the faint so sudden that he had no opportunity to put his arms out to stop his fall. He broke his nose and smashed his jaw in three places. He was hospitalised for three weeks with his jaw wired shut for two of those weeks. When he came back to Trentham he was under instructions to be careful about undertaking any physical activity which pretty much ruled out everything we were doing. He had also missed almost a month of classroom work.

This was his downfall. He was only an average student at the best of times and the backlog of work turned out to be too much for him. His marks fell below the required grade for the end-of-term exams and he was unable to pass a special catch-up exam he was given. This left the police no option but to dismiss him from training. I believe, in the end, the fall not only broke his nose and jaw but his spirit as well.

THE RAFT OF DEATH

The potential for injury during training at Trentham was high. We were regularly pushed to our physical and mental limits and something had to give. Normally it was an ankle or a knee, but sometimes it was much worse. I remember seeing one cadet in tears after being told he had torn the cartilages in his knee. An operation was required and he was afraid he would be thrown out of training. Heartless though our instructors were, they didn't stoop so low as to throw out a cadet who'd been injured in the line of duty and he received the convalescence he required, with no threat of expulsion.

Obviously our instructors had an obligation to weed out those of us who might crack under stress and it was better to find out who couldn't hack it at training stage, but I do question some of their methods. Especially their attempts to kill us at least once a term.

They were careful to disguise these attempts on our lives as 'team building exercises' but I wasn't fooled. Whenever the phrase was mentioned a cold shiver would creep up my spine.

The first of many such exercises was given the seemingly harmless name of 'the raft race'. The objective of the race was for each section to build a raft and float it down an 8km stretch of the Hutt River. Sounds innocent enough but there were several catches.

First of all, we were given no equipment to build our rafts. Our instructors allowed us one week to beg, steal or borrow the materials we needed to construct our floating masterpieces. This meant all sorts of odds and ends were gathered together as potential raft equipment - unfortunately much of it chosen because of its accessibility rather than its buoyancy.

We were also encouraged to race competitively.

It was to be our first inter-section challenge and our platoon leaders put a lot of pressure on us to not only win the race, but to destroy the other rafts in the process. It was made clear that the race would have no rules and almost anything was allowed. This included bombing and sabotage.

I had already gained a reputation as an agent of destruction (usually unintentionally) so I was put in charge of our raft's armaments. It was a task I undertook with relish. I decided the most effective way to turn our floating death-trap into the Nimitz would be to mount a beer-can bazooka on the starboard bow.

I had never made a beer-can bazooka before (and wasn't sure where starboard was), but this didn't deter me in the least. You see, I had the knowledge. Recently, a mate from New Plymouth claimed to have constructed a mortar capable of firing a milk bottle over a barn. Naturally I pestered him for the plans and in the end he told all, though subsequent events suggest he left out a few pertinent details.

According to my mate, all I had to do was cut the top and bottom out of two beer cans and attach them to an empty third can, which was complete but with the tear tab removed. Glad wrap was placed over the open tear tab and the three cans were taped together. A small hole was then drilled in the side of the third can, into which lighter fluid was poured. When half full, a paper wick was stuffed into the hole and the bazooka was primed for firing. The intended projectile was then inserted into the barrel formed by the top two cans. The wick was lit and whammo, everything within an 80km radius was decimated. At least that was the theory.

It seemed perfectly logical to me, so I was quite surprised at the turn out for my test firing. Word of the impending explosion spread like wildfire and a sizeable audience gathered (at a respectable distance) to observe the proceedings.

I was reluctant to expose my section's secret weapon to all and sundry so I decided to use a different accelerant for the trial run. My reasoning being if I used petrol instead of lighter fluid the weapon wouldn't perform to its full potential but would still put on a good show. Besides lighter fluid was hard to come by and I figured one flammable liquid was pretty much like another. At this stage I should probably remind everyone I failed science at school.

To say the launch was a complete failure would be untrue, as many of the audience went away very pleased, especially those from other sections. I must admit that the beer can bazooka didn't live up to the hype. The idea was to launch the assorted rocks and twigs I'd tipped down its barrel over the Gumbies barracks; instead it blew up in my hand. I sustained major damage to my credibility as an explosives expert and minor burns to my person. All the hair was burned off the back of my right hand and one of my eyebrows took a minor singeing.

Thinking back, I can't figure out how I believed it would work in the first place.

Amazingly, I didn't lose my position as armaments officer after the misfire but it was suggested that I concentrate on less ambitious forms of weaponry, such as flour-and-water bombs. These I could make, and by race day I had assembled an impressive array of surface-to-raft missiles, including a few eggs I'd nicked from the cookhouse.

Our raft looked magnificent. The lads had successfully scavenged several empty 44-gallon drums and lashed them to a couple of lengths of wood. We had high hopes for race day and approached the starting line with our victory speeches already prepared.

The race started well with the C section raft, more than holding its own in the opening flour-and-water barrage. Several of our eggs found their mark and even without our bazooka we were a raft to be feared.

Sadly our moments of glory were short-lived. After the first 100 metres things began to unravel or, more specifically, our raft began to unravel. Of all the damnable luck, we'd constructed our raft before we learned how to tie knots properly and our sheep shanks turned out to be pig's ears.

We tried to keep our rapidly disintegrating raft together but knew after half a kilometre that it was a lost cause. We floundered about in the shallows for several hours, clinging to a bit of sodden rope and our one remaining drum. By this time the other sections had finished the race and we still hadn't made the halfway mark. In the end the instructors took pity on us and hauled our cold, bruised and bedraggled bodies out of the water.

Our humiliation was only made bearable when we heard that one other hapless crew had to be rescued as well, and their failure, though not as complete as ours, was possibly even more embarrassing. They had taken an early lead in their sleek inner tube and wood raft but soon discovered a major design fault. The six-inch nails they used to join the boards together had gone through the wood and when they hit the first set of rapids the nails punctured the inner tubes. They sank like a stone.

B section took out the race, followed closely by A section and, thanks to our abysmal effort, C section came last.

Aside from contusions and several doses of the flu no permanent injuries were sustained in the raft race.

Just when we thought the rigours of inter-section competition were behind us, we received a nasty surprise. No sooner had our bruises turned from black to yellow than the next team-building exercise was announced. It was time to start preparing for the trolley race - just like the raft race but on dry land, and much, much, more dangerous.

In this endeavour we would be hurtling down a steep slope in a cart, which again we had to build ourselves. Naturally, this filled the members of my team with much joy given the outstanding success of our home-made raft. Suffice to say we were put in charge of strategy rather than construction.

Only one trolley was required per section this time and we

were given five days to find the materials and make the carts. Then, on the given day, we were to select a pilot and race the section cart down a yet-to-be named hill.

The instructors showed great cunning in leaving the venue unnamed until after the drivers were selected, because no one in their right mind would have volunteered had they known the location. With the benefit of hindsight it should have been obvious that the sadistic bastards would choose a venue capable of delivering maximum carnage. But we were still relatively unblooded and clung desperately to the mistaken belief that our instructors wouldn't let anything really bad happen to us.

The venue for the trolley race was the water-tower hill. The same incline we had been forced to run up and down after the Gumbie water fight. Except, this time we would be travelling down the other side. The frighteningly steep, virtually inaccessible part, containing the worst hairpin bends. This would have been scary enough had it been a grass or dirt track. But no. The path they chose was covered in gravel. Nasty, skiddy, treacherous, dig bloody great holes out of your knees gravel.

Of course we didn't know this as we built our trolley. Still, the level of danger for our unselected pilot increased daily as our cart began to take shape. Unfortunately, it didn't seem to be taking the shape of a cart. It quickly became clear no-one in our group had even the most basic knowledge of physics or mechanics. To put it bluntly, our trolley was an ill-constructed, dangerous, piece of crap.

The steering device consisted of a mangy bit of old rope

attached to the cart's front wheels and the braking mechanism was a wedge of wood that the poor sod who was driving was supposed to kick between the wheel and what was loosely called the chassis.

The only safety feature our instructors insisted upon was that none of the trolleys were to be powered by anything more than a good push at the top of the hill. This was a small mercy because, had petrol been involved, I'm convinced half of Trentham would have been engulfed in a fireball of molten metal and smouldering cadets.

Astonishingly, the other section's carts were not much better our sad machine. Some of them had brakes that looked like they might actually work, and one section had gone to the trouble of painting their cart but, all in all, it was a pretty decrepit array of vehicles that parked at the top of the water-tower hill on the day of the race.

The sections had drawn straws to choose their drivers the previous day. This gave the condemned men a chance to make their peace with their gods and contact their loved ones before the race began. The selected men moped around the barracks like they were walking the green mile, except for our driver. His name was Keith and he was surprisingly optimistic about his chances - but then Keith was surprisingly optimistic about most things. He was one of the few cadets who believed we were fortunate to be the last wing through Trentham because he'd been told the hardships we faced on a daily basis would prepare us for life as a beat constable. Bollocks to that. The only reason we were still in Trentham was because it made the police budget go further and the minister would look good come the end of the financial year.

Still, we did nothing to discourage Keith's sunny outlook. We figured that if he approached the race feeling like he had a possibility of coming out alive then there was a chance, however slight, that he might cross the finish line in pole position, heaping glory upon himself and the section as a whole.

Our hopes were misplaced. Within the first 20 metres Keith deftly steered over a bank and the only thing left of him - and the cart - was the brake wedge sitting next to a skid mark at the top of the cliff. It took 10 minutes to untangle him from the wreckage, by which time A section's cart had crossed the finish line. One of B section's wheels crossed just before Keith's stretcher and, in a hotly contested decision, they were awarded second place.

C section were last again but we knew revenge would be sweet when it came. The problem was that it would be a very long time before that day arrived.

While a great deal of emphasis was placed on the physical aspects of police training most of the day was taken up by more mundane matters. Like learning the law.

The task of teaching us the basics of policing fell mainly to our section sergeant. He was the most important person in our lives for the following 12 months.

Your section sergeant held total control of your destiny. He ran our day to day programme and was required to report on our individual progress each term, effectively deciding who passed and who failed. If your sergeant deemed your attitude inappropriate then you'd have to a pretty exceptional trainee to still be around for the next term.

Your sergeant was your teacher, your adviser, your confessor, your friend (occasionally), your enemy (more often), your personal trainer, your spiritual guide and sometimes even your mother, though naturally that was never admitted aloud. Accordingly, it was a damn good idea to get on with him.

Our sergeant's name was Rodney Edwards and at 29 he was the youngest section sergeant at Trentham. To say he was a bit of a character is an understatement. I vividly remember the first day of our course when Sergeant Edwards introduced himself. He strolled into the classroom and to get our attention, slammed what I took to be a baseball bat into the desk. It worked! In less time than you could say 'Al Capone' we were sitting upright and facing the front. The offensive weapon he had bashed into the desk turned out to be nothing more dangerous than a sawn off pool cue, but Sergeant Edwards wielded it like a ninja. He could dint a dozing cadet's head from thirty paces away and have it back in his hand before the swelling started.

To be fair, Sergeant Edwards seldom used the cue to inflict injury; he used it more to illustrate a point. And illustrate points he did. Sergeant Edwards had more points than a starfish menage a trois. He had a theory for everything and every time he expounded one of his philosophies he punctuated the salient themes by pounding the fat end of the cue into the nearest desk. This not only ensured we remembered the point he was making but also guaranteed no-one fell asleep in class. Not that this was likely to happen because Sergeant Edwards made even the most complex pieces of law interesting. He was a fascinating teacher because he was able to illustrate every lesson with highly embellished stories from his time on the beat. He made a mockery of the old adage 'those who can do, those who can't teach'. He did and he taught.

Sergeant Edwards was exactly the type of instructor we needed. He was strict when he needed to be but could also identify with us on our own level. He had the respect of every cadet in our section and I'm certain his unorthodox teaching style and approachable manner were responsible for many cadets sticking with the course where they might have otherwise packed it in.

An example of his ability to engender team spirit came on the first day. He shared his nickname with us, a small thing but it set the tone for the coming months. His nickname was 'Jacko'. We never found out why, though we tried to on an almost daily basis.

This disclosure had an unfortunate spin off for me. Naturally once 'Jacko' had revealed his deep dark secret, the rest of the cadets set about uncovering old or making new nicknames for everyone else in the class. I felt I was safe though. I had sworn Goose to secrecy and was confident of finally getting rid of the Gonzo tag I'd carried around for the last ten years. Unbelievably, it was not to be. It happened like this.

A cadet several rows in front of me was one of the first to be singled out for a new nickname. Everyone looked hard at the guy trying to single out a physical characteristic or mannerism they could mercilessly exploit. Then some joker yelled out 'Hey he looks just like Fozzie Bear from the Muppets.' There was more than a passing resemblance and everyone started laughing. The poor sod (whose real name was Greg before it became lost forever) jumped indignantly to his feet and cried out 'I look about as much like Fozzie Bear as he does Gonzo.' He was pointing directly at me.

Goose burst into hysterical laughter, which didn't help my cause, but by then I knew the fickle hand of fate had once more slipped inside my underpants and given my testicles a firm squeeze. That was it: I was Gonzo again.

The nicknaming of section C continued throughout the week and by Sunday everyone in the section was covered. These names were, of course, a moveable feast and several cadets had many nicknames before the end of the year, some names reflecting moments of great bravery but more often, incidents of extreme stupidity. Some of the more creative names in the section included Pig Pen, Disco Kid, the Prince of Darkness, Dipstick, Captain Beekey, Duggy Wuggles and Shag.

The tallest cadet in the section was known as Big Jim while his best mate, and coincidently the shortest member of the wing, was called Little Jim. The section's worst swimmer became "Aquaman" and two cadets of Dutch descent had their family names bastardised. Mark Van Der Kley became Van Der What and Craig Van Dugteren was forever after known as Van Doiger Doiger. Isn't it comforting to know the people who invented these names are now patrolling our streets?

As you'd expect from an organisation such as the New Zealand Police our routine was set within the first week of the course and was extremely regimented. Breakfast was at 7am, followed by inspection and parade at 8.00. then we had to be in class by eight thirty.

Things were so strict at the start that we were required to march in formation both to and from meals. This was seriously irritating because it meant you couldn't elect to sleep in rather than have breakfast. I'm not a 'morning person': my idea of a good sunrise is one that doesn't involve me.

We studied law for the first part of every day, then had a break for lunch and were back in the classroom for general studies in the afternoon. General Studies was a new concept in policing and was one of the few courses taught by civilian personnel. It covered the more psychological aspects of policing rather than hard-and-fast rules of law. The topics covered were pretty heavy, and valuable though they may have been, we had little time for this course. It was hard for the majority of us cocksure cadets to imagine the stress the job would put on our health and mental stability. We were 18 years old and we were invincible. The concept that pressure from the job could rip marriages apart was hard to grasp when our idea of a steady relationship was if you called back for a second date.

Boredom wasn't a problem during training as the police

ensured our days contained a healthy sprinkling of things to look forward to. Periods we enjoyed included self defence and physical training, practical policing demonstrations, sport, weapons training and quite a few other activities, which I'll put into the category of miscellaneous cool stuff. Generally any activity that involved shooting, driving, blowing things up and trips away from Trentham fell under this umbrella. The training was intense and by the end of the day we were knackered.

Our class work mostly finished at 4.30 and we had a free hour before dinner at 5.30 (I think the only people in New Zealand who ate that early were police cadets and rest home residents). I use the term 'free' in the loosest possible way, as there was always something to prepare for the next day. There was ironing to be done or law to swot, or shoes to polish and we frequently had to make up our rooms again after a midday snap inspection.

We didn't have much time to ourselves during the first term: even Saturday mornings belonged to the police. We were required to be in class from 8am until noon to revise our weekly work. For 'revise', read 'be tested upon', because almost every Saturday contained a 'surprise' test. So regular were these supposedly unexpected tests that we were amazed if a Saturday went by without one. The police use the word spontaneous only on carefully planned occasions and I suspect they even had a written schedule for their random raids.

Our bosses deigned to give us the rest of the weekend off, providing we were back on base by 10pm on Saturday and Sunday nights. This restricted our social lives considerably but we were nothing if not resourceful and regularly found ways of getting into trouble.

I felt most sorry for fathers of teenage daughters in the areas of Trentham and Upper Hutt. Every year there would be an influx of 80 fit and horny young men who were suddenly away from their regular girlfriends and keen to liaise with the locals. These Dads learnt from bitter experience that aside from locking their daughters in the cellar it was nigh on impossible to keep the cadets away from them and vice versa. So they clubbed together and come up with a cunning plan. Within the first week of our arrival we were invited to the Upper Hutt hall for a 'social dance' with the locals. This enabled the fathers to get a good look at the bunch of deviants who'd arrived in town for the sole purpose of impregnating their daughters. It also gave us the chance to work out who we wanted to impregnate, and the girls got to choose who they'd like to be impregnated by. A good system all round.

You didn't need to be a genius to figure out that no untoward behaviour would be tolerated at the dance itself. The security was too good. Fathers started cleaning their chainsaws if you even looked like touching their daughters while dancing and the mothers hovered around like a cloud of angry bees. A relaxing evening it was not. Still, we did enjoy the female company and against all odds a few dates were arranged for the following weekend.

As I was still in madly in love with Carey, I was able to stare temptation straight in the face and tell it to naff off. Not that a lot of temptation actually came my way so my reserve wasn't truly tested. But like any man, I had complete confidence in my ability to remain faithful when not faced with any other option. So far I'd only spent one day with Carey and it was getting monotonous professing undying love via New Zealand Post (no texting or email back then!). This was, however, our only option as she was based in Palmerston North, almost a three-hour drive from Trentham, and out of bounds at any time other than leave weekends.

These precious weekends allowed cadets to escape from Trentham on Friday night and not return until Sunday night. They were the only glimmer of hope on bleak romantic horizons and we looked forward to them with a passion. But there was only one leave weekend in the entire first term.

Why didn't I just sneak out for the weekend after Saturday class you may ask? For two very good reasons. Firstly, cadets were not allowed to have vehicles at Trentham during the first term which made it bloody difficult to get anywhere. And secondly, there was a nightly inspection just to make sure every cadet was tucked up in his own bed. This check was done whenever the duty inspector felt like it so it was impossible to plan an escape. If you were caught not in your bed then you were immediately declared Absent With Out Leave and subject to instant dismissal from training.

A few cadets still found the possibility of a bonk so irresistible that they tried to beat the system. Most escapes occurred in the second term when the rules had been relaxed but even then it was still a risky venture. One cadet used a window dresser's dummy head in the place of his own one night and got away with it but the most memorable deception featured none other than my mate Quentin.

For some inexplicable reason Quentin had woken up one night in his flat in Palmerston North and decided that it would be a good time to hitch around the South Island. It was the middle of winter and apparently he'd got as far as Blenheim, ran out of money and realised that perhaps he should have packed a bit more than just his father's old coat before setting off.

So now he was penny less in Wellington, on his way back to Palmerston North, and desperately in need of a place to stay. He was at my mercy and where Quentin's concerned, I don't have any.

Remembering all the times he'd been 'the sensible one' I decided this was too good an opportunity to pass up so I suggested he stay in the police barracks with me. He was a bit surprised and asked me if I thought the police would mind. I said they probably would if they knew but we weren't going to tell them so it wouldn't be a problem. I outlined my plan.

One of the other cadets was very keen to get out for the night but needed covering, so I suggested that Quentin sleep in his bed. The cadet, whose penis was well and truly in the driving seat, readily agreed and Quentin was out of options, so I set it up. I neglected to mention that he was required to be in bed when the duty sergeant came around. Or that he would be required to mimic the cadet's voice and reply "here" if the sergeant so required. They did this sometimes after they got wind of the dummy incident. I left telling Quentin these vital pieces of information until it was too late for him to back out and by bedtime he was in a right state. It hadn't helped his calm when a few of us informed him of the penalty for impersonating a police officer but the best moment came as he was preparing for bed. We told him the name of the cadet who he'd be impersonating - Rangi Waratene, one of the Maori cadets. Quentin's face went a peculiar colour and he stammered 'But I'm white!'

I told him he looked more greeny-orange to me and walked off, chuckling loudly all the way back to my room.

According to Rangi's room-mate, Quentin went straight to bed and hid under the covers for the remainder of the night, though he could be heard practicing muffled Maori phrases under the blanket.

Fortunately the duty Sergeant only made a cursory check that evening and Quentin's incomprehensible mumbling didn't arouse any suspicion.

Quentin has yet to see the funny side of the incident and claims to have been emotionally scarred. He says he sometimes wakes up late at night sweating and shouting out "Kia ora" at the top of his lungs. His wife refuses to confirm or deny this story.

ARMED AND DANGEROUS

In case you were wondering, here are the main aims of the New Zealand Police (which I find disturbingly similar to the prime directives of Robocop):

To protect life and property.

To prevent offences.

To apprehend offenders

To preserve the public peace

So now you know.

And while I'm in the mood for disclosures, here's one that may surprise you. Amongst the equipment a Police Officer is advised, nay required, to carry is ...a crayon. So when he is confronted by an armed maniac he can yell 'Drop your weapon immediately or I shall be forced to draw a hopscotch outline on the pavement.'

As you can see this book is not afraid to make the tough calls and take you deep inside the seedy world of modern law enforcement, which brings us neatly to the General Poananga, 24th Cadet Wing's first field trip. Where do you think our kind hearted instructors decided to take us?

The zoo. No.

The park. Not on your nelly.

Stock car racing. Nup

They decided to take us to the mortuary to see an autopsy being performed. I was dreading it. I was extremely squeamish and my biggest concern about joining up had been whether I'd be able to handle the blood-and-guts side of the job. I didn't have a good pedigree in this area. When I was a kid I didn't do as much fishing as I would have liked because I couldn't stand gutting fish. Still can't, I don't mind catching them, but there's no way I'm going to cut them open. These days my friends realise how sensitive I am and do the yucky stuff for me. I have an arrangement with my brother-in-law whereby he gets half the catch, if he guts and scales my share as well.

My mates at school weren't nearly as understanding. I remember a bunch of them chasing me around the house with fish hearts still beating in their nasty little hands. It was like something out of an Edger Allen Poe novel and it's a wonder I grew up to be the well adjusted adult I am today.

C Section was scheduled to visit the mortuary last and Sergeant Edwards was making the most of it. He spent the entire week telling us dead body stories that increased in grossness and became more graphic as the dreaded day approached. I was disturbed to discover that not everybody shared my concern. Some cadets were actually looking forward to it.

A and B sections were to visit on Monday and Tuesday and C section was to go on Thursday. By Tuesday night the barracks were rife with stories of rib cutters and skull saws. According to eye witness accounts rib cutters were huge scissor-like implements that could chop through the rib cage in three easy cracks. One member of A section was able to mimic the sound the disgusting tool made perfectly and he regaled us with details over dinner. He was able to give an impressive reconstruction of the whole surgical process courtesy of a couple of chop bones and some tomato sauce. I felt quite woozy by the end of his performance.

Skull saws were in a different league altogether. Their effects were discussed in hushed tones by small pockets of cadets huddled in dark corners around the barracks. It seemed this incredible surgical tool was similar to a hand held circular saw and its spinning blade was used to slice through the bone at the top of the skull, cutting it open like a knife through the top of a boiled egg, as one cadet put it. The stories got worse with tales of skin being peeled off the skull and brain oozing out all over the place. I didn't stick around to hear the really gory details as I had to get to the bathroom urgently.

So far the instructors had been disappointed with the cadet casualty tally. From the first two sections they only had one vomiting, one full faint and two partial faints, however they were expecting big things from C Section - and from me in particular. Imagine their disappointment when the hospital phoned on Wednesday afternoon to say there had been an outbreak of Legionnaires Disease in one of the wards and the hospital was under quarantine. All visits were cancelled. Woo hoo! Saved.

Our instructors had to be satisfied with first-aid classes instead, in which they got to show us horrible car accident movies and slides of burn victims. At least the room was dark and I was able to hide behind my hands during the yucky bits, which turned out to be nearly the entire course. Even with my fingers providing shelter I could still hear the soundtrack and caught the odd unavoidable glimpse of munched-up human beings. This proved too much for me and by the end of the first showing I had to be sat by the door. By the end of the second day (drownings), I was seated outside the door where I could draw in big gulps of fresh air to stop from keeling over.

I was quite worried by this time and had convinced myself I'd be dropped from the course for being such a wuss. I'd be hopeless as a policeman if every time I attended an accident I took one look, and spent the rest of the evening standing in the background hyperventilating into a paper bag.

I told Sergeant Edwards my concerns. He was great. He took me aside and said he had the same problem in training but when he got out onto the streets and had to deal with the blood and gore first hand he found he was too busy to worry about feeling sick. He told me people look to you to take control of the situation so you just have to grit your teeth and get on with it no matter how you feel. He also assured me that after I'd seen a few bodies I would become desensitised and it wouldn't worry me as much. I had my doubts, but if he was confident I wasn't going to argue.

My other main worry about the course was keeping up with the RFL's (required fitness levels). Our fitness was tested when we first arrived and another was scheduled for a few days after the first aid course. I had sustained minor damage from the beer-can bazooka and the abortive raft race but was in pretty good shape.

In my first RFL I finished in the middle of the pack and I felt my fitness was coming along nicely. The Police drove us very hard physically, with gym work and runs or tramps every day. I was also playing rugby for one of the police teams and was training after class at least twice a week. Sergeant Edwards was my coach and I was looking forward to a good season. I was disappointed not to be in the top police team but was reasonably happy to be in the Second XV. I had been a good rugby player in my first two years at secondary school but had changed position in my third year and hadn't got to grips with the new spot. Originally I played hooker and loved it but I had to move out of the front row when I grew taller than the props. Now I was trying flanker, number eight or lock and didn't know where I belonged.

On the rugby field as elsewhere, the spectre of injury hung over my head. Dad always said I stuck my head where most players wouldn't put their boot and I often came out of a game more battered than the other players. This wasn't due to exceptional bravery on my part - more an inability to get out of the way of danger.

Fortunately the high level of fitness forced upon us in the police was working in my favour and to date I was injury free, which boded well for our second RFL. This time I wasn't the one who was struggling. One of the guys from our section was finding the going very tough, especially the 2.5km run. His name was Mark and he was a hell of nice guy, the sort of bloke who'd do anything for you no matter how much it put him out. He was big but a touch overweight, and the few extra pounds he was carrying were causing some problems. He was struggling with the sit ups and chin ups but the run really worried him.

Mark had failed the first RFL and it was made clear that if he didn't pass this one he was out. His generous spirit and easy going nature made him very popular and no-one in the section wanted to see him fail so the fittest guys in the class set up a rigorous training schedule for him. These guys gave up what little spare time they had to work with him. It was amazing to watch everyone get behind Mark; whenever he was training the Section was always there egging him on. On the day of the RFL we all gathered around and cheered loudly every time he completed a push up, sit up, or pull up. We were willing him on and it seemed to give him strength. It was obviously hard for him but he did the required amount of repetitions in the requisite time.

Now came the run.

In what I can only describe as an astonishing display of teamwork, every cadet in the section sacrificed their own RFL rating to run with Mark. Not a single cadet passed him on the track that day. We ran alongside him encouraging and pushing him for every metre of the course. He was shattered when he crossed the finish line but he'd done it in his personal best time and had passed the RFL. And because he was under the required time we all passed as well. It was the most selfless display I have ever seen. What made it momentous was that normally we were such a highly competitive bunch of bastards. There were always petty little battles being fought to see who was the fastest, the strongest, the smartest, the fittest, had the biggest penis etc, but that was all put aside for this one brief but memorable moment.

This story should end happily but this is real life and it didn't. Mark's personal best wasn't good enough for the police and even though he'd improved in his first two fitness tests they failed him a month later after the next RFL. It was decided that his improvements hadn't been great enough and he was asked to leave the course. We were devastated. In his own way Mark had been tougher than all of us put together. He had faced an uphill climb right from the start but he stuck at it with guts and determination. What's more he did it without complaining or blaming anyone but himself. We all thought the police could have given him another chance as he was exactly the sort of cop they needed. I know why they failed him; the demands on our fitness got tougher and tougher as the year progressed and there was no way the rest of us could have continued to help him the way we had. It was hard enough getting ourselves through, let alone anyone else. Selfishness, it appeared, was one of the lessons we had to learn to become police officers.

With the second RFL out of the way we were ready to get on with our next challenge and this one definitely fell into the 'cool stuff' category. It was time for the cadets of C Section to be unleashed on the rifle range.

Finally we were getting to the things I'd joined up to do. We were about to get tooled up and boy, was I looking forward to it. Our batons and handcuffs were still a term and a half away and the most lethal things we'd been exposed to so far were the cookhouse potatoes.

I'd done rifle shooting before as my school ran an army training course. I shot really well in that exercise but it may have been a fluke because I only just scraped through at Trentham. I really enjoyed shooting but was unable to do much more than give the paper Nazi soldiers I was aiming at a nasty fright. I did manage to do quite a bit of damage to the Nazi next to my guy. I was informed this was not the aim of the exercise. I suggested that even though technically I hadn't hit my Nazi, I had inflicted an enormous psychological damage on him. After all, he'd just seen his best mate cut down in a hail of bullets and would be in counselling for years. My argument was rejected and I was given another magazine to see if I could do some actual damage to him. This time I blew his paper butt away. We had a great morning on the range but the best part was yet to come. That afternoon we were to have a go at pistol shooting. A'right!

I'd never shot a pistol before but had watched a lot of Dirty Harry movies and was confident I could handle it.

Our instructors had set up a really cool course and we were excited about the prospect of an afternoon on the firing range. The course was arranged with three standing man-sized targets which were set up about 15 metres back from the firing area. They stood beside each other about 5 yard metres apart. Directly in front of them in the firing area were three square wooden shields of about the same size as the targets. This was our cover. About 20 metres away was a small wooden stake. We had to run around this between firing at the targets. The idea was to race past the wooden peg with your pistol loaded and holstered, then sprint to the first cover barrier, remove your pistol from its holster, take off the safety catch and fire three rounds at the adjacent target from a standing position. Once you'd completed your three shots you had to run back around the peg, return to the second firing area and fire three rounds at the next target from a kneeling position. Your pistol was now empty and you were to eject the spent shells onto the polythene beneath your knees, take cover, and load three fresh bullets into the chamber. Once reloaded you were to run around the peg again and return to the third firing zone where you could fire your final three rounds from a lying position. It wasn't until you got into the final position that you discovered how well you'd loaded the gun after the kneeling round.

It was really tricky because if you hadn't spun the chamber into the correct firing position then one of the following things would happen. If you'd spun the chamber too far the second bullet would fire instead of the first. Then the third bullet, then nothing, you'd hit an empty chamber. This left you with one rogue round in the gun. Bad. If you didn't spin the chamber far enough then your first shot would be a click as you again hit an empty chamber. Also bad.

Points were deducted from your score if a click was heard

where there should have been a bang. Points were also deducted if your bullets missed the target or if you took longer than two minutes to complete the course. You also lost points if you were unable to find all six empty cartridges from your gun (see the Arthur Allan Thomas case).

After you'd fired your final three lying shots, one last dash around the peg was required before you could return to the starting position with your pistol holstered and the safety catch on. It was a hell of a lot to remember and the time limit meant you had to squeeze off your shots quickly. The pistol shoot was going to be fun but it wasn't going to be easy to pass.

I was second up to shoot and I tore around the course like a madman. My standing shots thudded into the suspects vital organs no problems at all. I sent the second bad guy to meet his maker with my kneeling shots, emptied the chamber, reloaded and headed off for the peg confident that all was well. I got cocky as I approached the third target and decided to roll into the lying position, as I'd seen people do on many 1970's cop shows. I whirled on the grass with my weapon over my head and spun onto my stomach, then pumped hot lead into the last scumbag's groin. He wouldn't trouble the good folk of Dry Gulch again, no siree.

I was sure my fancy rollin' and shootin' had impressed the hell out of the instructor, so I sauntered back to the starting line, half expecting applause. Instead I got a right bollocking.

'What the hell was that?' the instructor shouted into my face from about 10 centimetres away. I was too shocked to answer. It appeared that as I'd rolled over, my gun had travelled in a wide arc around my head and everyone had to dive for cover.   I tried pathetically to explain that this was how Starsky did it and he'd never shot Hutch, but it was no use, I was in disgrace.

We were all given a lecture on the difference between real life and the movies and were informed that points would be deducted for any variations from standard shooting procedures. My misdemeanour would probably have been overlooked if I'd turned out to be a crack shot but sadly, out of the nine shots I'd fired only two had hit kill spots, five had done some minor wounding and two had missed altogether.

I had failed the pistol shoot. This meant I wasn't allowed to be armed as a police constable until I sat and passed a test at the station I would be sent to, assuming I passed the rest of training and graduated. It was a black mark on my record but only a minor one - several other cadets failed the shooting as well.

After we had finished feeding lead sandwiches to the paper crims we were taken aside for a lecture on firearms safety (a bit late, I thought). We had been shooting with standard issue .38s and though they gave a bit of a kick they were relatively easy to handle and we felt confident with the weapon. At least we did until the instructors began swapping stories. Our instructor had been on an Armed Offenders call-out to a gang confrontation, when things got out of control. As the trouble reached its zenith one particularly large gang member broke ranks and charged the police lines. He was brandishing a large kitchen knife. He was warned to drop the knife several times but just kept charging so our instructor shot him in the leg. It didn't make a jot of a difference; in fact it just seemed to piss him off. So our instructor shot him in the other leg. This slowed him but he didn't stop completely until a dog took him down. They found out later he was high on drugs and booze and didn't even remember being shot. After that the Armed Offenders squad made sure they had quick access to bigger calibre guns.

This story was a lead-up to our instructor's next trick and he pulled out a .357 magnum (a bloody big gun). He then picked two 'volunteers' to shoot the pistol. Phil and I were selected. I held the pistol in a relaxed manner, concentrating on the target not the kick of the gun. This thing exploded like a cannon, snapping my wrists back and sending the bullet way above where I was aiming. I was relieved to see Phil had the same problem and was also rubbing his wrists. Once our instructor finished smirking, he came over and showed us how to brace properly. My second shot hit the target and I was seriously impressed at the size of the hole I'd made in the paper guy's chest. But not half as impressed as I was when our instructor fired the same gun at a piece of sheet metal. The bullet punched right through it. Cool.

Several other weapons were on display that afternoon. I'm not a gun nut so I can't remember exactly what they were but I was very impressed by the carnage they inflicted on the various tin cans, water containers and wooden targets that were our opposition for the afternoon.

New Zealand Police 573, Paper Nazis 0.

Best of all, at the end of the day our instructors snuck off early, leaving us to pick up the cartridges and collect the targets. This meant we were able to dig around in the dirt banks behind the range to find the heads of the fired bullets. I found one in almost perfect condition and was certain it was one of my shells. After all, most of the bullets I'd fired weren't impeded by hitting anything so they were bound to be undamaged.

Being the sentimental old romantic I am, I decided to steal a cartridge case, mount the head back on it, shine it, get it engraved, put a chain on it and give it to Carey. You should have seen the look on her face when I presented her with a beautiful bullet pendant inscribed with the tender words 'To Carey, you blew my heart away, from Glenn.'

Nothing says 'I love you' like ammunition.

LAW & DISORDER

Three very important events were looming. The Fleetwood Mac concert, our first leave weekend and first-term exams.

The reason I was excited about Fleetwood Mac had nothing to do with the band. I thought they were cack and musically they represented everything I detested (although Stevie Nicks was quite cute). But, Carey liked them and a group of teachers' college students were coming down from Palmerston North for the concert. Conveniently the event was on a Friday night and our only leave weekend of the term fell on the Saturday and Sunday. This meant I could go to the concert with Carey then grab a lift to Palmerston North for the next two days. Only one thing stood in my way. I was sitting on two bookings. One more and I'd be confined to barracks for the weekend.

The crimes I'd committed to put me in this sad position were particularly heinous. I was given my first booking because the windows on my side of the room were dirtier than Rob's.

My second offence was leaving my togs neatly rolled up on my bed instead of put away in my drawers. I regarded this as particularly stink booking as the only reason I hadn't put them away was because I was rushing to my next class, so I wouldn't be booked for lateness. Miserable gits.

I was very worried as the leave weekend was only two weeks away and it was extremely unlikely I'd last a fortnight without being booked.

There was only one thing to do. I was going to have to get myself booked immediately and sacrifice the weekend before the leave weekend. It should be easy enough - at this stage of the course we'd get booked for breathing funny. I decided not to blot my copybook too badly - I would get caught for the minor, but highly bookable, offence of walking around with my hands in my pockets. This was a sure-fire winner. Every instructor in the camp kept an eagle eye out for such lapses and had their pen out before you could say, "I was just scratching my testicles, sir."

I walked around every inch of Trentham for two whole days with my hands stuffed so far into my trousers that I should have been arrested for obscene behaviour, but do you think I could get booked? No way. It was as if every instructor had suddenly gone blind. The other cadets knew my scheme and they couldn't believe what was happening. The booking blitz continued as usual, but no matter how blatantly I flaunted this most basic breech of the dress code, I could not get punished. Then one day the chief inspector (God himself) spotted me slouching around outside the classroom, pointed at me and yelled 'You, Cadet, come over here.'

This is it, I thought, I'm booked for sure. But no, he just wanted to send me on a pointless errand. Unbelievable!

To cap it off, when one of the instructors did finally notice my transgression, he let me off with a warning. No one got let off with a warning; it was unheard of. he other cadets were gobsmacked. I instantly became the luckiest, unlucky bastard in the camp.

81

In the end I gave up and booked myself. I made up some offence then reported that I now had three bookings. It never occurred to the instructors that a cadet would purposely book himself so they didn't check the entries and I was confined to barracks for the weekend before leave.

It was horrible. I spent the entire time ironing, spit shining, reporting for inspection and cleaning various things that didn't need cleaning. It was boring in the extreme and to rub salt in the wound I got booked again for having railway tracks (two crease marks instead of one) on my shirt sleeve.

At least I had company in the barracks. One of my mates was on his third confinement in a row. His nickname was Pig Pen and it doesn't take a genius to work out what he kept getting confined for. He was one of those guys who is just naturally messy whereas his room-mate, Wayne, was a compulsive cleaner. They were the police's version of 'the odd couple'. Pig Pen's half of the room looked like a bomb site but you could've eaten off the furniture on Wayne's side. Quite often you'd enter their room to find PP lying amongst a pile of dirty laundry reading a Penthouse while Wayne was on his side spit polishing his already gleaming shoes. Yet despite this, or maybe because of it, they got on well and their room was a popular port of call for me and my mates.

I got through the rest of the weekend without any further bookings and faced a nervous week sitting on one booking but knowing it wouldn't be hard to pick up two more.

Fortunately, come Friday night, I had survived the week and was free to spend the evening with Carey and (unfortunately) Fleetwood Mac. From there I was off to Palmerston North for a weekend of sleeping on the floor of Quentin's flat and dodging the Matron at Blair Tennent Hall, where Carey was in residence.

Blair Tennent was the home to 78 girls aged between 17 and 19, all of whom were away from home for the first time. I'd discovered its joys the year before while visiting friends. Quite simply it was paradise. My friend was going out with a girl who lived there and we went round to visit her. It was 8pm and already a number of the girls were in their night attire and those that weren't were still, well, women.

It was too much for me, a shy young boy from Taranaki who had never seen more than 12 women in one place, and that was the Girls' High school choir. The whole experience was quite surreal, it was like the scene from the Monty Python movie The Quest For the Holy Grail in which Sir Galahad the Pure had entered the castle Anthrax to be confronted by a bevy of young virgins wanting to be spanked. Admittedly, not many of the residents of Blair Tennent looked interested in a spanking and I don't think the virgin count was very high, but I stand by my analogy.

I blushed from head to toe the moment I entered the hall, then completely lost the ability to speak. Instead I sat around making pathetic mewing sounds until I was thrown out by the matron.

Being matron was probably the worst job in the world. Her role was to chaperone the girls, all 78 of them, keeping them away from boys and alcohol. And what are the two things the majority of 18 year old girls want? That's right, a hot cup of Milo and a good book.

Obviously the only option open to this poor woman was to run Blair Tennent like a Russian Gulag. She was forever throwing boys out onto the street and banning them from ever darkening her doorways again. I was biffed out a few times during the year for not sticking to visiting hours (who would have thought 3am wasn't acceptable?), but managed to avoid actually being banned. Which was fortunate as Blair Tennent was Carey's home for the whole of my year at Trentham.

The Fleetwood Mac concert, despite my misgivings, turned out to be extremely cool. The band had a massive argument on stage and stuffed up playing their instruments because they were all so mad with each other. I thought it improved their songs immensely. In the end they stormed off stage and didn't return until their manager said if they didn't finish the set they wouldn't get paid.

This was good because it gave Carey and me a bit of unexpected cuddling and snogging time, much to the disgust of her assorted friends and work-mates. I don't normally go in for public displays of affection, but we had to make every moment count as we'd be separated again soon. We were in that sickly, 'first couple of months of the relationship' stage where common sense is overtaken by infatuation and our behaviour was truly vomit-inducing. Still, we were probably the only two who enjoyed the Fleetwood Mac concert, so what the hell.

The show ended on a high note too: I saw my first sucking chest wound.

It happened as we were leaving the venue. Just outside the gate we came across a guy who had been stabbed in a fight and he was lying on the ground doing a lot of bleeding. The St John's Ambulance people had arrived first and were trying to keep the guy alive until the hospital ambulance arrived. I wandered over to see if I could help.

They had everything under control but I got a good look at the guy's injury. He had a 3cm horizontal cut on the right side of his chest. The knife had gone in deep and punctured a lung, which was causing the wound to suck. It made a whistling sound and the blood was pink and frothy. I was fascinated as we'd just studied this in First Aid, and there it was happening right in front of me. The guy who had been stabbed didn't seem to share my excitement and the St Johns people suggested I'd be more useful doing crowd control. I didn't get a chance to do much because the 'real' police arrived and told me that what I thought was crowd control was just me getting in the way. I can take a hint so I made a graceful exit and rushed back to the girls to describe the guy's stab wound in minute detail. When one of them asked me to stop because she felt sick I realised that, amazingly, I didn't. This was great news.It seemed Sergeant Edwards was right: I'd been so focused on trying to help that the sight of blood hadn't fazed me at all. I was so pleased I decided to relate the story over again. I walked back to the car by myself.

The rest of the weekend was spent testing Carey's moral fortitude and I'm sorry to say she passed with flying colours. Apparently it was best if we took things slowly. This was a blow to me, as my plans were to take things as fast as possible, but she was in the driver's seat and clearly we weren't going to take the car out of first gear.

Still, we were going in the right direction and I figured it was just a matter of time before her foot came off the brake. I didn't really mind as I was just as happy (well, almost as happy) simply enjoying female company for a change. The only women at Trentham either outranked me, fed me medicine, or were attempting to teach me to type, so our conversations were somewhat limited.

The weekend went way too fast and before I knew it I was back at Trentham. Not everyone made it back, though. One guy decided enough was enough and hadn't returned from leave. I'm sure he wasn't the only one who considered it. The leave weekend served to remind us what we were missing and the thought of another nine months of snap inspections, extreme physical and mental pressure, and oppressive discipline, was enough to cause even the most determined cadet to waver.

The pressure was on in the classroom too. Our first-term exams were only a month away and we were told if we failed we were out. There was no pussyfooting around with wimpy 50 per cent pass rates either. The police required a 70 per cent minimum mark to pass.

I was doing quite well on the weekly tests, with good results in most subjects. So far I had received 78 for General Orders, 72 for Beats, 71 for Statements, 77 for the Coroners Act, 83 for our second test on Statements, 87 for the Children and Young Persons Act, 80 for the Mental Health Act. And I scored 73 in a general first term-test which was a warm up for the big exam.

I was pleasantly surprised by my marks as my school work had always been average. I only just squeaked through School Certificate, failing maths badly (having to take Taranaki Certificate Maths, or 'thickie maths' as my classmates unkindly called it) and had to spend two years in the Sixth Form before I got University Entrance. Mind you, Quentin was in all my classes for the first year, which didn't help. To say we didn't really apply ourselves is an understatement. Quentin should have flown through UE but only made it by the skin of his teeth and I missed out by ten marks (that 32 for Biology didn't help). So, to be getting marks in the seventies and eighties was a novelty for me.

My interest in the subject matter made a big difference. At school I didn't really give a stuff what crop the farmers of the mid-west of America planted in their fields. Perhaps if the answer had been opium I might have paid attention. But it wasn't, it was corn, and I fell asleep.

Now I was learning about cool stuff, like this gem from the statutes related to death.

It is not an offence to attempt to commit suicide. The law is only broken if you succeed and then you can be charged.

(Okay Mr Dead Guy, you've really done it this time. Boy, are you in trouble.)

I also found legal definitions most interesting. For example, the definition of domestic violence is as follows;

"Violence is conduct, verbal or non verbal, which will damage the recipient, physically, socially, intellectually or emotionally. Damage means to hinder normal growth or development or to divert it into deviant behaviour."

Actually the lecture on domestic violence was both fascinating and frightening. Of all the incidents a police officer attends, the most dangerous by far is a domestic dispute. That's because you never know what is going to happen next. If you are attending an armed robbery you are at least aware that the offender has a weapon and have prepared yourself accordingly. In a domestic situation anything can and does happen.

This was driven home in the most chilling fashion when our instructor told us the first rule for attending a domestic dispute. Never park your patrol car in front of the house or property concerned. This became standard procedure after two constables pulled up outside a house that had been subject to a domestic dispute call. The guy inside the house had just killed his wife and he shot both cops before they even opened the patrol car doors. They died instantly.

Law was fine but sometimes theory got beyond us. Fortunately Jacko was always there to translate. Here is a segment from a thesis we were supposed to read on the Children and Young Person's Act;

'West (1965) groups these theories under the general rubric of "social protest" theories: that juvenile offending is a protest or reaction to existing inequalities within society. The results produced in this report are entirely consistent with this interpretation in that rates of juvenile offending reflect what would appear to be lines of stratification in New Zealand society with those groups in the most advantaged position displaying a low rate of juvenile offending and those groups in the most deprived positions displaying a high rate of offending.'

There were 22 pages of this stuff, which Jacko would sum up by saying;

'Poor kids get locked up more than rich kids. It ain't fair but it's the way it is.'

He would then elaborate with a colourful story from his time on the beat in Wairoa and we wouldn't have to read all the dull guff.

I did have a few problems on the academic front.

My biggest area of difficulty was spelling. I am slightly dyslexic and have never been able to grasp the fundamentals of technical English. I scored 26 out of 50 in my first-term spelling test. Hot on the heels of my appalling spelling was my abysmal typing. I was by far the worst in my class. I have quite big hands and they are not suited to a typewriter keyboard. Several other cadets had similar problems but none shared my complete lack of co-ordination. It was bad enough when I was looking at the keyboard but my over-eager typing teacher was always trying to get me to type with my eyes fixed straight ahead. I ended up with sentences like this: 'The wuick browm nox bumoed ocer the jazi sog.'

I just couldn't get the hang of using all 10 fingers to type. I'd get all fumbled up and my speed would drop from 20 words a minute to 6. In the end she gave up and let me look at the keyboard and type with whatever fingers I liked. Then she failed me.

Before our main exams we had to sit first-aid exams. I was heartened by the sucking chest wound incident and was sure I'd manage to stay conscious long enough to pass. Happily I was right and got good marks. I even managed to save the life of the plastic CPR dummy with the paper-bag lungs. Back then we were taught to use a pre-cardial thump on patients who had stopped breathing. This involved whacking your fist in the patient's chest area before starting mouth to mouth resuscitation. Later in the year, while on station duty, one of the cadets used this method on a guy who had stopped breathing. He got the guy's heart going again, thanks to CPR, but broke two of his ribs with the pre-cardial thump. That particular practice is no longer considered effective (i.e. do not try this at home.)

Dad was particularly pleased I passed first aid, as he was a qualified medical officer at the wharf and had been trying to show me the basics for ages. Normally I was the patient. He spent most of my teenage years strapping up strained ankles, icing bruises and stopping me from bleeding to death. I guess some of the things he showed me must have stuck.

The first-term exams were split into four sections: law, general studies, Practical and typing (uh oh). The law exam covered police powers involved in dealing with the mentally ill, the Children and Young Persons Act, deaths, prisoners' rights and the Coroners Act.

General Studies covered the rights of suspects and offenders, the causes of domestic disputes, police procedures in these areas and communications skills.

The practical part of the exam took us out of the classroom and onto the streets of Trentham. We would be placed in a series of mock situations and marked on how we handled them. Our instructors or fellow cadets would play offenders or victims and we would do our best to bring the situation to a satisfactory conclusion. From there we were expected to complete the appropriate paperwork and hand it in for marking.

I really enjoyed the practicals because they were a chance to apply what we'd learnt in the classroom in 'real' situations, except, as I found out later, these 'real' situations were a long way from real 'real' situations. It was unlikely your fellow cadet or instructor would punch you in the nose if you took the wrong approach.

I hated the paperwork, though. There were so many forms to fill out and they all had to be completed to strictly controlled formats. The wording had to be exactly the same every time and there was no room for creative interpretation. I found this very frustrating as I love playing with words and thought the existing police reports could do with a bit of livening up. I was not, however, foolish enough to try to improve the existing formats during the exams.

We sat our examinations on the 21st and 22nd of April 1980 and had to wait three whole days before we found out our results.

YOU'LL NEVER TAKE ME ALIVE

My marks were 88 for law, 78 for general studies, 72 for my practical and 48 for typing. I was taken aside and spoken to about my typing result. I was informed I had to get my results above 50 per cent for the next exam. Sergeant Edwards didn't make a big deal out of it though. He said no cadet had ever been thrown out of Trentham for being a crap typist. That was a relief.

However, Sergeant Edwards was unhappy with the section's results in general. He was grumpy and sulky when he passed out our paper, saying he thought we could have done better. He wanted us to be the top section but we fell somewhere in the middle. The majority of us had passed, so I think he was being a bit unfair, but it still took him a couple of periods to accept we weren't the geniuses he wanted us to be.

Three of the cadets had failed the exams and were asked to leave Trentham, their careers over before they had started. Others who failed were given a reprieve through the chief inspector's discretionary power, as it was felt they could improve enough to pass the second and final exams. The cadet's attitude, popularity and physical accomplishments were taken into account when this decision was made, and these candidates were aware they were on borrowed time.

It was hard on everyone when a cadet was dismissed from

training. For three months these guys had been our friends, our room-mates and people with whom we'd shared the rigours of training with. It reminded us of our own vulnerability.

Those of us that were left had earned a break. We'd survived the first term and had just one more task to perform before we received a week's leave. It was an assignment we were looking forward to - station duty. For three whole weeks we were going to be (almost) real cops. The idea was to send us back to our home towns to work under the supervision of the local police.

This was well cool. We'd be wearing our uniforms for the first time in public and although we had no actual power of arrest we would be in the real world, protecting and serving with the best of them.

The only way Joe Public would be able to tell we weren't real cops would be by our hats, which had a plain white band instead of a chequered band. A removable white band, though it would be a brave and probably unemployed cadet who would take it off. We also had the word 'CADET' emblazoned on our shirt epaulettes instead of a number but it was hard to see and invisible if you were wearing your jacket. Besides the public never looks closely at cops, all they see is a uniform. And they seldom question if the person telling them what to do actually has that right.

The next day Goose and I were on the bus home. Great, another six hours of Bob Marley. Tragically Trentham hadn't shaken Goose's Rastafarian faith. If anything he'd got worse and was often heard muttering about growing dreadlocks when training was over.

94

He certainly had no chance of that at Trentham. If your hair even looked like growing, the clippers came out. This was a bit of a shock for me, as prior to Trentham I'd been sporting a rather fetching afro hairstyle. Well, I thought it was stylish; my wife informs me it looked gormless. I remain unconvinced as I was considered something of a style guru in my younger days.

Mum and Dad were pleased to see me (they had to be, I was their son). Dad had hidden his illegal booze and Mum fussed around cooking things for me. This was actually a good idea because the police had made the classic mistake of letting us select our own meals, buffet style. This meant no-one was around to make me eat vegetables, so I didn't. For the past three months I'd eaten nothing but roast meat, potatoes, bread and gravy. Occasionally, very occasionally, I would make a small sacrifice for health and include a tiny spoonful of peas, but that was it. For lunch I'd create my own masterpiece, the pie sandwich. This culinary delight involves placing a large meat pie between two slices of bread, adding tomato sauce, and then chowing down. It was a treat. I spent the entire year vege-free (except for when Mum got hold of me), and boy did I pay for it later.

On my first night at home my parents invited all our relatives around to show me off, which meant parading around in my uniform while they all went 'Ohhh doesn't he look handsome.'

Worse was to come. The next day the Taranaki Herald came to the police station to take photographs of myself and Goose. They had decided to do a story on our station duty. It made the front page (not a lot happens in New Plymouth), which meant for the next three weeks all my friends also went 'Ohhh doesn't he look handsome,' but not with the same sincerity.

Actually it was quite a buzz being in the paper and even more of a thrill walking around town in uniform. I felt important and it was interesting bumping into people who had seen me just the year before as a loser second-year sixth schoolboy. Now I was a cop. Suddenly they perceived me differently. I now had the power to deprive them of their liberty if they pissed me off (I couldn't of course but they didn't know that).

It was a weird feeling being out on patrol for the first time - exciting but kind of scary too. We didn't attend any major incidents in my first week, just routine burglaries, drunk and disorderlies, car thefts, suspicious persons, that kind of thing, but I found it fascinating to be putting what we had learnt in Trentham into practice.

On the other hand, the New Plymouth cops found it annoying. If I was to point out, for example, that the correct procedure for dealing with a young offender caught shoplifting was to take the suspect into custody, fill out a notification form 333 and place him in the care of a youth aid officer - rather than giving him a clip around the ear and phoning his Mum - then the local boys got a bit narky. But they were generally pretty good. They could see that Goose and I were full of youthful exuberance and were doing our best to make a good impression.

New Plymouth isn't the wildest of towns and it wasn't until the end of the second week that I was involved in an incident that bought home the realities of the job. I was working a late shift in the I Car (incident car - first called to all major events).

It had been a quiet shift and we were just about to break for dinner when we were called back to the station. There had been an accident on Mt Egmont (this was before it became Mt Taranaki). We were briefed on the situation and directed to New Plymouth Base Hospital to await further developments. It seemed two young climbers had got caught in a blizzard and one had stumbled over a bluff falling about 50 metres. His condition was not known, but because of the length of the fall and the rocky area he had fallen into it didn't sound good. Search and Rescue were on the scene and would be either attempting to save the climber or retrieving his body, depending on what they found. We were to stand by at the hospital and help out where we could. After about an hour we received the call that a body had been found and was being flown back to the hospital mortuary. We were to wait there and receive the corpse.

I was dreading it. I had never seen a dead body before and had no idea what to expect. I'd heard the other cadet's mortuary visit stories but nothing could have prepared me for what I was about to experience. We arrived about five minutes before the body did and a big silver table was being scrubbed down in preparation. A doctor and two nurses were dealing with the sterilisation of the equipment, but they weren't very chatty and got on with their work, almost completely ignoring us.

The doctor's job was to confirm that the victim was dead and the nurses were to assist in cleaning up the body. Our job was to take possession of any valuables that may be still on the corpse and then find out who he was and get the body ready for identification by his relatives. Thankfully we wouldn't be breaking the sad news to his family, which, in my opinion, is the worst job in the police.

The cop I was with was one of the older guys and he was winding me up, though in a good-natured sort of way. I think he could tell how nervous I'd become and was trying to make light of the situation. Humour seems to be the most common method cops use to deal with death. When I first saw police joking around a body, it seemed ghoulish and insensitive, but after a while I realised it was a coping mechanism that allowed them to do their job without any lasting psychological damage. As soon as a corpse becomes personalised it immediately forces you to deal with the fact that it is someone's son or daughter, mother or father, brother or sister, friend or lover and it's human nature to delay that moment for as long as possible.

My time had finally arrived and without warning the body was wheeled through the mortuary doors on a battered old hospital trolley. The corpse was contained in a large canvas body bag, which had been packed in at the accident site. The body bag was in very poor condition - it was dripping wet from the ice and snow and stained and bloody. I didn't want to go anywhere near it. This wasn't an option and I was called over to help unzip the bag, remove the corpse and move it onto the newly scrubbed trolley. I held the bag firmly as the other cop unzipped it. The first thing I saw was a ragged hole in the middle of the victim's forehead. His skull had been smashed open and the pulped interior of the brain was exposed. It was a gory sight and I felt horrified, but at no stage did I feel like fainting or vomiting.

As we stripped the body and cleaned it up, the thing that upset me the most was the man's age and the lack of other injuries. He was a fit and healthy man in his mid-twenties – not much older than me, and he could easily have been one of my mate's older brothers. I didn't know him, but that didn't make his death any easier to take. There were a few bruises on his legs but from the bridge of the nose downwards he was in almost perfect condition.

The huge hole just above his eyebrows left no question as to how he died. He must have taken the full impact of the fall on that one spot, in the centre of his forehead. Perhaps he fell on a rock - I don't know, but whatever happened he wouldn't have felt a thing. Death would have been instantaneous and at least that was a blessing.

The hardest job was trying to make the body look presentable for identification. A great deal of care went into displaying it in the most sympathetic way. The nurses cleaned the edges of the wound and we warmed up the body so it wouldn't look so blue and cold but there was very little we could do to hide the hole in the dead man's head. In the end we covered the top of his skull with a sheet so his relatives would only see him from the eyes down.

The police may be insensitive bastards behind the scenes but

I've never seen any cop be anything less than professional, understanding and supportive, when dealing with a bereaved family.

I was present when the boy's father identified the body and it was one of the saddest moments of my life. He didn't break down or cry; he simply nodded his head and walked away. Not in an uncaring way - the devastation he was feeling was painful to witness – I think he was just overwhelmed by the hopelessness of the situation. There was no doubt it was his son and he was clearly dead. It was cruel and final.

After he had left I felt completely and utterly drained. I hadn't cried and wouldn't allow myself to. This was my job from now on and I knew that I would either deal with these situations or they would destroy me.

At the end of the night the senior officer back at the station took me aside and told me I'd handled myself well. It was good of him to say so and I appreciated it, but somehow his praise fell flat. I just wanted to go home.

Goose heard about my experience the next day and was keen to know all the details. Suddenly I had an edge. I was the most experienced cadet of the two of us as I'd handled a death. I played down the incident and made out I'd just been a bystander, which was close to the truth. Back in Trentham however, the story would grow to include me flying the rescue helicopter in gale force winds while steering with my teeth then winching the body off the mountain single handed.

For his part Goose had been in a fight and witnessed a couple of arrests. By the end of the second week I'd say we were even on the 'who'd had the best station duty' stakes. I edged ahead in the third week by getting my photo in the newspaper again. Goose was well pissed off. It happened like this.

Two days before going on leave, my shift decided to have an Armed Offenders exercise. All they needed now was an armed offender. Guess who?

I was rapt. They drove me to a deserted farmhouse, gave me a rifle plus heaps of rounds of blank ammunition and told me to shoot anything that moved. This was more like it. I was armed and dangerous. They waited until we arrived before telling me that three squads of highly trained killers and two tracker dogs would be sent after me. Foolishly unfazed, I set about barricading myself in the house, determined to go out in a blaze of glory.

The layout of the farm was as follows. The main house had two bedrooms looking out onto paddocks at the front of the section. The land was scrubby, but there was bugger all cover out that way, so I ruled it out as a possible attack point. The lounge area looked towards the east, which again was surrounded by paddocks, though there was a hedge and a few trees, making it a more attractive proposition for attack. I pinpointed this as the most likely line of approach for the squad. To the rear was the toilet and laundry then, about twenty metres away, was a tin garage and a woolshed. My plan was that after I'd blown away a squad or two, I would make my escape into the barn, then blast my way out the side window into the bush beyond. Then I'd live on the lam for a few weeks before finally making it over the border to Mexico.

On the west side of the house was the kitchen. It looked directly onto several large piles of firewood and general rubbish, just beyond that was a huge gully with a roaring river in the middle. There was no way anyone was going to approach from that direction. My plan for the first half hour was simple: I'd run from room to room looking out all the windows until I spotted something, then I'd shoot it.

I didn't have to wait long. I saw a couple of guys moving behind the trees so I fired several rounds out the lounge window. It would have been impossible to hit them from that distance but I wanted them to know they'd been seen. As soon as the shots were fired the figures hit the ground and disappeared. Jeez they moved fast. I watched the spot where they had dropped for about five minutes but couldn't see a thing. I had no idea where they'd gone and it made me jittery.

They'd moved up to the trees pretty quickly so maybe they were coming in from other areas as well. I ran around every window straining my eyes for movement. I was now utterly in the role of the crazed offender trapped by the pigs in his own house with nowhere to run. My adrenalin was pumping and I was determined to take out as many of them as I could. It was frightening now to think how quickly it became a 'them or me' scenario. I shudder to think what it must be like in a real siege situation.

I moved out the back for a quick look around in the yard, just to make sure my escape route was still clear. As I stepped onto the rear steps a dog handler appeared at the corner of the garage. I fired two quick shots and retreated into the house.

How the hell had he got so close so fast? And where was the rest of his squad? Shit, if he was around that side of the garage they'd cut off my escape route, unless I ran for it. No - that must be where the rest of the squad were, in the barn. Goddamn it.

My head was spinning. Where had they come from? I'd been watching that side of the house like a hawk! I couldn't think. I ran to the lounge window and fired at shadows. Suddenly I had an overwhelming desire to get out of the house. I was trapped like a fart in a sleeping bag.

I knew it was only a matter of time before they stormed the place so I decided to fool them. I'd duck out the side door, hide behind the wood pile and shoot them through the kitchen window from the outside. They'd never expect that. Then, once confusion reigned, I'd escape down the gully and take my chances in the river. Brilliant.

I must have exited through the side door just as they stormed the back of the house because seconds after I hit the woodpile I saw a couple of cops appear at the kitchen window. Holy Crap they'd moved fast. I was blown away by how efficiently they'd taken the place. But I think they were expecting a firefight inside the house and were looking a bit confused at the lack of shooting.

'Right,' I thought, 'I'll fix that,' and I opened fire at the coppers in the window. They got a hell of a shock, but nowhere near the fright I got when I rolled on my back to reload and stared straight down the barrel of a very large rifle.

'Drop it,' yelled the person holding the gun.

I damn near shat myself as another fifteen guys with rifles appeared and pointed the guns at my head. I dropped my weapon immediately, all thoughts of going out in a blaze of glory evaporating.

At this point I expected the Armed Offenders guys to say 'Okay gottcha, well done lads' and we'd all have a jolly good laugh. No way, this was serious stuff and as the squad leader covered me one of the other guys ran at me and pushed me roughly onto the ground. I felt handcuffs being slapped on my wrists and before I knew it I was being searched. As they held me on the ground the two dog handlers came over and let their dogs have a go at scaring me to death. Both Alsatians were straining at their leads, trying to take a chunk of me while their handlers held their jaws just out of biting distance. Apparently this was making a very good photo (such a relief that my absolute terror wasn't for nothing).

After they'd roughed me up for a while the squad leader kicked me onto my back and said 'Okay, set the dogs on him.' My heart stopped. Then I heard him laugh and someone took my cuffs off. After that we were best of mates (so I wouldn't sue) and we started the debriefing.

It was one of the shortest exercises they had ever had. Normally the offender barricades himself in the house and they have to smoke him out. They were disappointed that they didn't get to gas me but what the hell, there was always next time.

Apparently the uncrossable gully wasn't, and a squad of Armed Offenders had traversed it to surround the house from the west. My best escape route, it seems, would have been the barn as they hadn't been able to cover it by the time I left the house. Typical isn't it - if I'd stuck to my original plan I'd have been drinking Margarita's somewhere over the border instead of lying face down in the dust covered in dog spit.

The next question was the most important – 'how many cops had I shot?' I said I would definitely have plugged the dog handler (which brought about much hilarity as apparently he gets shot on every exercise), and I would probably have taken out the two cops in the window as well. They nodded soberly and wrote a new page in their operations manual entitled 'What to do when faced with an offender who has never had a logical thought in his life.'

The photograph appeared in the paper the next day, a quarter-page picture of me spreadeagled and handcuffed on the ground, surrounded by armed police and barking dogs. The caption read: 'Few people would have enjoyed being in a situation similar to the one staged by members of the Armed Offenders Squad at Inglewood this week. Twenty-five squad members from New Plymouth and Palmerston North are at present in Taranaki conducting regular combined exercises, which are held every three months. The squad has held manoeuvres at both Stratford and Inglewood. Squad members are pictured here while staging a mock search of an armed offender. Police Cadet Len Wood (Len??) was apprehended, handcuffed and searched by Constable Don Allen. At the ready was dog handler, Dave George and another armed policeman.'

The famous Len Wood or, as I've been known to the tax department for about 15 years, Glenn Kenneth Wodd. This is despite numerous letters informing them my name is actually Glenn Keith Wood. Once they actually replied: 'Thank you for helping correct our records, Mr Widd, we'll make the appropriate changes immediately.'

Nothing else of consequence happened for the remainder of station duty, and the time came to relax and enjoy our hard-earned leave. I was travelling to Palmerston North for the rest of my time off to try and persuade Carey that she needed a few more driving lessons. And speaking of driving, in a less metaphorical sense, I was just about to buy my first car.

One of the major concessions the police were made for our second term of training was that we were allowed to have vehicles. The only snag being that I didn't actually own one, not unless you count the Kawi 100, and I didn't.

I had saved some money during my first month of training, due to the fact that we were too busy to spend it. So I decided to add it to my savings and get a decent car. Snag number two, I didn't have any savings. This was because I had worked at Jim's Foodtown for two years after school, being paid the princely sum of 99 cents an hour. It was daylight robbery but I got no sympathy from my parents. Dad said that if Jim had deducted all the stuff I damaged from my wages then I'd end up having to pay him.

Anyway, what it came down to was a bank balance of approximately $800. Not, you would have thought, enough to buy a car. Wrong. Dad had a mate who was prepared to let me have a perfectly serviceable vehicle for that exact amount. He would be taking a loss, of course. Cutting off his arm. It was a once only offer and although it pained him to let such a magnificent machine go for such a ridiculous price, he'd given his word and a deal was a deal. I finally agreed to have a look at this majestic example of precision engineering after being informed that he thought of me as the son he'd never had. Besides, beggars can't be choosers, and I really, really, wanted a car.

Actually, calling it a car is unfair to every other member of the automobile family. Yeah, it had four wheels, a couple of doors, a roof and was propelled by what could, at a stretch, be called an engine, but there the similarities ended.

It was a Mini and it was pink.

I mentioned these obvious flaws to Dad but he just shrugged and asked me what else I'd seen in my price bracket. He had a point. Car dealers weren't exactly sending me hand-delivered invitations to come to their yards. But still, a pink mini…

Dad said it was up to me and in a cruel, but remarkably effective move, jingled the keys to the Kawi 100 under my nose. Suddenly the Mini started to look a bit bigger and not quite so pink. More of a light orange from some angles and it did have black pinstripes down the sides. The seat also went way back so I could almost get my knees under the steering wheel. And learning how to double the clutch was a driving skill lost to many drivers these days. And it was cheap to run. And I really, really wanted a car.

The more I thought about it the better ideas it seemed.

If I owned a time machine and could travel back to one particular moment in history to stop myself doing something incredibly stupid, this would be it. But I don't and I bought the damn car.

I called it Floyd because it was pink and I thought that was quite witty. Once Carey stopped laughing she said she thought it was witty too, but I think she was humouring me as I'd obviously had some kind of a breakdown.

Quentin was less sympathetic and refused to have Floyd parked in his flat's driveway. He said it clashed with everything he owned. I quickly replied that was okay because there wasn't enough room due to all the other fabulous vehicles parked there (one rusty 10-speed). After this stinging attack he relented and let me park it round the back.

The enormity of my error didn't strike me until I returned to Trentham. There was no question who had the crappiest car in the wing and the Gonzo legend began to grow.

THE THREE P'S

Winter was coming. We knew this because our instructors began organising a one-mile swim through Wellington Harbour. I'd never swum a mile before and it sounded like a sod of a long way. And to cap it off we would be swimming in freezing temperatures.

This was obviously another team-building exercise; several weeks had gone by without our being placed in mortal danger and our instructors clearly thought that was too long. Just to spice up our harbour swim and give it an extra edge of danger, we would be swimming right past the meatworks outlet. A favourite dining area for sharks.

I am terrified of sharks. The movie Jaws had a profound and lasting effect on me. In fact I hold Steven Spielberg partially responsible for destroying my promising marine biology career. I decided having a limb ripped off by a massive shark, just to protect the breeding place of the greater speckled puffer fish, was not the job for me. The puffer fish could fend for themselves.

So, to recap: we would be swimming a mile through Wellington Harbour, past the shark-infested meat works, in sub-zero temperatures. Well, that would certainly prepare everyone who survived for life as a beat constable.

Those of us who couldn't swim would bloody well have to learn. That was our instructor's directive as we began training in the Trentham pool.

A mile was approximately 100 lengths of the pool and we were tested on the first day to see how many we could do. I swam 40 lengths which was about average. No one made the full 100 but a couple got close.

Godfrey Watson, a mate of mine, almost made one length without sinking. The instructors thought he was having them on. He wasn't. Godfrey (instantly nicknamed Aquaman) is without doubt the worst swimmer I have ever seen. He is completely unable to float. He was promptly taken aside for special swimming training.

We had three weeks to prepare for the swim and by the end of that time almost everyone was able to swim the 100 lengths. Aquaman had managed six, thanks to probably the most patient instructor in the whole college. In the end even this sainted instructor snapped. After Aqua failed to make it across the pool without a flutter-board for the 20th time in five minutes, his instructor walked round to where Godfrey was thrashing about in the shallows and yelled 'Watson, you have the buoyancy of a brick shithouse.' Then he stomped off in disgust.

Aqua was told he wouldn't be taking part in the harbour swim. He was really disappointed but most of us would have traded places with him in a flash.

Our bus arrived at the diving-off point on a grey and cold Wellington morning. The instructors were in fine spirits. They were so happy that before letting us disembark they walked around the bus surfing their hands past the windows like shark fins, the jolly wags.

To help protect us from the cold our instructors supplied us with a large jar of Vaseline. It gave them quite a laugh watching us smearing it all over our bodies, with most cadets paying particular attention to an area of the body which has been known to shrivel in cold water. The thought that there was even the remotest possibility of permanent shrinkage was more than any self-respecting male could bear.

Once we were all greased up we had to leap off the dock in groups of three, made up of a good swimmer, an average swimmer and a poor swimmer. The aim of the exercise was to get every member of the group home.

My group was close to the front, for which I'm grateful. We only had to listen to a few screams of pain as warm bodies were suddenly immersed in freezing water. Hearing the continuous gasps of shock must have been really demoralising for the groups at the end of the line.

Hitting the water was like being slapped in the genitals with a frozen trout. The Vaseline had no decernable effect and the only way to warm up was to swim like buggery. There was an upside to this freezing my bollocks off though; I had completely forgotten about the sharks.

My group kept up a steady but unremarkable pace and we finished in a reasonable time with only minimal discomfort and shrinkage.

About two-thirds of the cadets who entered the water got out under their own steam. Cold and exhaustion took its toll on the other third and they had to be rescued by police patrol boats. Phil was among the rescued - he got bad cramp in his leg half way through the swim. No one was eaten by a shark. I think they could sense that we had a lot of suffering ahead of us and to have been slaughtered so early in the term would have been the easy way out. Cruel creatures, sharks.

Quite a few cadets got sick after the swim (what a surprise) and this was when we discovered Molly's Mixture. Molly was Trentham's resident nurse and she dispensed her own medicine, which quickly became legendary. It wasn't very effective but it contained a copious amount of alcohol - half a bottle of MM and you were drunk as a skunk. And as it was a prescribed medicine we had a legitimate, unbookable excuse.

The instructors figured out what was going on after about two weeks, when large numbers of intoxicated cadets were reported lurching around the barracks, swigging from brown plastic medicine bottles. Sadly, Molly was taken aside and told to tone down her brew: the flu was never as much fun after that.

The police were very strict on the alcohol consumption while we were training. Of course, they realised that they couldn't stop 80 teenagers indulging in the occasional drinking binge, but they made it clear that if we were caught under age in a pub or dinking illegally in a public place then we would be in serious trouble. Fair enough: in 12 months' time we would be expected to arrest people for doing the same thing. Not that we thought about actually becoming police officers. Few of us believed we would make it through second term, let alone graduate.

It was during one of these bouts of post-swim illness that Sergeant Edwards asked to borrow my car. Naturally I thought I was delirious; no one had ever shown anything but complete disdain for Floyd, and Jacko had laughed loudest when my recent purchase was unkindly discussed in class.

Efforts to justify my vehicular decision had failed very early on. I invited one of the most vocally sceptical members of my section for a drive so I could prove Floyd wasn't as bad as appeared. The cadet agreed, hopped into the passengers seat, shut the door and the side window fell onto his lap. Once I was able to be heard over the laughter, I explained it only happened occasionally and most times the window just slotted right back in again. But it was too late, the damage was done.

It seemed Sergeant Edwards was truly desperate. The other cadets were on a run and he needed to get into town urgently. His wife had his car and I was the only one around with car keys. I was rapt, this could restore Floyd's reputation. My plan was instantly foiled, Jacko swore me to silence under pain of extra PT, low test marks and a couple of unjustified bookings.

As I handed over the keys I remembered that it was my Carless Day (due to a petrol shortage the government had allocated all drivers days when they were not allowed to use their car and stickers identifying the banned day were placed in car windows. Driving on these days was an offence). I mentioned this to Jacko but it didn't faze him in the least - he claimed that his errand was a police emergency and the car was exempt from all restrictions. I made a half hearted attempt to get reassurance that he would pay any fines he received. Sergeant Edwards replied 'Only the speeding tickets,' then laughed all the way to the car.

He was back three-quarters of an hour later and looked shaken. He tossed my car keys on my bed and shook his head in what I like to think was admiration, but suspect may have been pity. 'Cadet Wood,' he said, 'you are either a very brave or very foolish young man.'

I replied I knew Floyd was less than ideal but I was desperate. He asked if there was a woman involved and I told him about my long-distance romance with Carey. He said he understood and walked away with a curious look in his eye.

A few days later Sergeant Edwards delivered his most memorable classroom speech. He spent an entire morning warning us about the dangers of the opposite sex. He wasn't against women - far from it - but he felt it was his duty to point out (very graphically) the many traps involved in dealing with the fairer sex.

It was the closest I saw Jacko come to preaching. He took to the subject with a religious fervour, frequently banging his pool cue on desktops to reinforce a particular point.

He started with a discourse on the three most common reasons for a young constable to be thrown out of the police in disgrace. These reasons were summed up as 'The Three P's' -

Property, Pricks and Piss (obviously none of the P's stood for Politically Correctness).

We were dutifully copying this down in our notebooks and were taken aback when Jacko told us to put down our pens. He said what he was about to tell us would not appear on any test. It was advice he was passing from one cop to another. His conspiratorial tones had us hanging on every word. This was no longer an instructor telling a group of cadets some indisputable point of law; this was some of the lads getting together over a few beers to chat about women. Choice.

Jacko elaborated on the three P's one at a time. 'Property' was defined at any item handed to you as a police constable. This included lost property given to you by the public, and stolen goods recovered from criminals to be used in evidence.

Sergeant Edwards emphasised the importance of properly recording and checking property when you received it. Receipts had to be issued and he impressed upon us the importance of personally escorting and handing goods to the watch-house keeper. We were to ensure the constable on duty acknowledged, in written form, receiving the goods.

In short, Jacko was saying things go missing, so cover yourself. Many an honest cop has found himself up to his neck in brown sticky stuff because he couldn't prove he had handed over property that had subsequently got lost. While stopping short of questioning the honesty of his fellow officers, Sergeant Edwards did make it clear the only way to avoid finger-pointing was to do your paperwork properly and trust no-one.

The next two P's fell into slightly more dubious areas. It's important to emphasise at this stage that the views expressed here aren't necessarily those of the author (who would like to remain married).

The second P stood for pricks. It could just have easily have stood for penises but that didn't have the impact Jacko was looking for. He admitted that he would also use the second P to talk about women, but explained that 'The Two P's and a W' didn't sound as good. Jacko did point out that his advice was a little harsh on womanhood in general, as it seemed to slander any woman who became involved with a police constable. The main thrust of his diatribe was to alert us to the thousands of loose women out there just waiting to get it on with a man in uniform (not so I'd noticed).

Basically, bonking on duty was a no-no and against the law. If you were married, then rumpy-pumpy with anyone who wasn't your wife should be avoided. Having it off with suspects was dodgy in the extreme and it was inadvisable to give a witness a quick shag. Knobbing your fellow officers also led to problems and probably concussion if they weren't female.

It seemed almost any carnal act would instantly bring your police career to a crashing halt. We thought this was harsh and you could feel the testosterone level in the classroom hitting unheard-of levels.

Jacko called for calm and explained. Sex was fine (phew), but not while on duty and not with anyone involved in a case you were working on. He explained that temptation was often placed in the way of police officers and normally an ulterior motive was involved. Your impartiality could be called into question if your activities were discovered and your credibility destroyed.

Ethical issues aside, doing the horizontal mambo with someone who just fancies doing it with a cop leaves you wide open for problems. Jacko told us of several cases of rape that had been alleged against some of his colleagues.

He summed up, in the quote he became famous (infamous) for: 'Woman, Boy! They'll get you in a power of shit.'

The third P was Piss. Sergeant Edwards was talking about alcoholism and it was rife in the police. The life most officers live is like a cocktail - if I can use a drinking simile and I believe I may. Work as a police officer is made up of two parts stress to one part responsibility. Blend that with macho pressure, then add a dash of temptation, and you've got a very dangerous mix indeed.

Sometimes, Sergeant Edwards said, it might seem easier to take what you have to face every day as a constable if you fortify yourself beforehand. After a particularly hard day, a drink makes you forget all the shit you've just dealt with. Then of course there is Sunday School. Not, you may have guessed, the religious one. Far from it. Sunday School happened at the end of every week of night shift. Cops worked nights once a month and because it was the most exciting and stressful shift, it was customary to have a drink when you knocked off on Sunday morning. This was normally a serious drinking session and the pressure to attend was enormous.

The police force was a very male domain and if you didn't drink you quickly became an outcast. Drinking could become so much a part of life in the police that it began to take over and hence many a cop has fallen foul of the third P. Get caught drunk on duty and you were out; get caught drinking and driving and your career is severely limited; get drunk and start a fight and your card was marked.

Drink and you end up in trouble; don't drink and end up in exile, not much of a choice. The problem with the former was that your fitness, health and marriage could go as quickly as your liver.

Sergeant Edwards did try and finish his rant on a positive note saying if we used our common sense we should be okay. Easy for him to say. I haven't got any.

It had been a revealing morning and one we would all remember. We felt more than ever that Jacko was on our side. He treated us like colleagues rather than students and gave us valuable insights into the attitudes and feelings of the average beat cop. He took time to explain things rather than have us blindly following orders. This was his strength and his weakness. He had our friendship and respect, but by dealing with us on our own level he lost some of the absolute power the other instructors had.

A few days later we had our third RFL, I was feeling off colour due to having drunk a large amount of Cossack shampoo. I had made the fatal error of nagging a passing cadet for a swig of Coke from the can he was holding in his hand. Amazingly, he agreed and I took a greedy gulp. It wasn't Coke, it was hair shampoo. His Cossack container had sprung a leak and the nearest empty receptacle had been a Coke can.

I intercepted him on his way to the shower and he later claimed he misinterpreted 'Giz a swig' to mean 'Mmmm, please poison me with that mass of red chemicals you have in your hand, cunningly disguised as Coca-Cola.' After spitting a mouthful of sticky red liquid down the front of his bathrobe (served him right), I ran to the bathroom and washed my mouth out. It was too late, I'd swallowed a large quantity of the vile stuff and it made me burp up soap bubbles for days.

Needless to say, I wasn't feeling in top form for the RFL. I thought of calling in sick but you needed at least a compound fracture or evidence of recent heart surgery to get out of a fitness assessment. Shampoo ingestion would not cut it. So I pushed up, pulled up, sat up and threw up. When I explained that the pool of red vomit at my feet wasn't blood but shampoo, the instructor looked relieved and made me complete the assessment as punishment for giving him a nasty fright. I felt better for throwing up and ran my best time. It's a funny old world isn't it?

Life continued along as normal (or as normal as it got at Trentham), for the next few days then on the afternoon of the 29May we learnt that Sergeant Edwards had collapsed and been taken to hospital. He had suffered a brain haemorrhage and was unconscious.

We couldn't believe it: he'd been teaching us that morning

and had taken my team for rugby practice the night before. The police played down the illness, saying the hospital needed to do tests before they knew what they were dealing with. We were upset and worried but thought Jacko would be fine, he was fit and healthy and, well, he was Jacko.

During gym the next day one of the cadets from our section suddenly cried out and ran from the gymnasium yelling "He's dead, he's dead." We didn't know what was going on; we thought the guy had flipped out. Ten minutes later the chief inspector came into the room and announced that Sergeant Edwards had just died.

We were stunned. Jacko, dead, just like that. It was unthinkable. He was only 29 years old and had a wife and two children.

Jacko's death affected me deeply, I'm not claiming to have been closer to him than the other cadets, but without his particular brand of teaching I'm not sure I would have survived the first term at Trentham. He had a knack for putting things in perspective and stories of his time on the beat (though probably wildly exaggerated), made an extremely tough course seem worthwhile. He loved the job and he made us love it too. More than that, he was a friend, he taught me how to turn the right way in a tackle, he laughed at my car, he made me feel better about being a crap typist, he pushed me to learn when I needed it, he made me laugh and he invited the whole section to his home to relax and tell a few jokes of dubious quality. How dare he die.

We walked across the courtyard in complete silence then sat in our classroom in shock as we were told Sergeant Edwards had not regained consciousness from the coma he fell into the day before. A blood clot had formed in his brain causing a massive haemorrhage and if he had recovered he would have been a vegetable. It was better he died.

The doctors couldn't say what caused the clot but the police had a pretty good idea. Several years before taking the teaching job at Trentham, Sergeant Edwards had been seriously assaulted while on the beat in Levin. He had been on the beat one evening, checking doors, when someone stepped out of the shadows and smashed him over the head with a block of 4x2. He was knocked unconscious and left on the ground. The person who did it was never found.

The cadet who had the death premonition was the same guy who was later to pull a knife on his room-mate. Yes, he was still there, even into the second term, though he was under psychological evaluation and would soon be dismissed from training. The creepiest thing was there was no way he could have known about the death when he ran from the gym, as the chief inspector had come straight off the phone to inform us. We timed the cadet's exit from the gym back to almost the exact moment Sergeant Edwards died.

Sergeant Edward's funeral on the coming Friday would be a full police funeral with a strict Catholic service. This came as a surprise. Jacko must have been a practicing Catholic, though from what we'd seen, he had lapsed somewhat.

Once the details of the funeral had been explained we were

given the option of staying in class to talk about what had happened or leaving to deal with his death in our own way. I stood up immediately and walked from the classroom in silence. It wasn't an act of rebellion: I just had to get out of there. The last thing I felt like doing was talking about the great times we had.

I wanted to be alone and I wanted to be miserable. This is how I deal with the death. I go off, have a good cry, mope around feeling sorry for myself, work up a heap of self-pity and immerse myself in misery.

I am a selfish mourner: I utterly refuse to believe anyone is suffering more than me. This makes me a pain in the arse at funerals but I get away with it because no one is going to say 'Snap out of it, you self-indulgent bastard' while I am grieving so obviously and publicly.

I went for a walk by the river, and I heard later that after I'd walked out everyone else followed. The whole section was suffering badly (though none as much as me). We hadn't lost an instructor; we'd lost one of our own. I stayed at the river until it was dark. I cried a lot and got angry, but nothing helped so in the end I went back to the barracks. No one said anything when I returned. There was nothing to say.

I hated the funeral. The priest spent the whole time talking about God. I didn't want to hear about God - it wasn't his funeral, it was Jacko's. The service was too long and the mood wasn't sad enough for me. Several of the cadets from our section formed a guard of honour and when they took the coffin away it finally dawned on me that he was gone.

There would be no more parties in Jacko's room.

THE WORST CAR IN THE WORLD

Our new section sergeant was a priest. In fact, he was the first ordained minister ever to teach at Trentham. Talk about from one extreme to the other. His name was Senior Sergeant Hanley and he had a big job ahead of him.

We were expecting the worst, but Senior Hanley took over an extremely hard job very well indeed. He didn't try and be a mate like Jacko. That would have been doomed to failure. Instead he taught the class with a no-nonsense attitude that gained him our respect early and he showed a very dry sense of humour, which we were quick to appreciate.

What endeared him most to me was that his car was even crappier than Floyd. He drove a Skoda: the only car lower on the food chain than a pink Mini. Even better, he was proud of his car and took a considerable amount of ribbing with dignity, refusing to respond to our criticisms.

Senior Hanley's approach was exactly what we needed. Sergeant Edwards's death had turned our world upside down and if we hadn't been handled properly we could have had a great deal of difficulty with the rest of our training. If our new instructor had treated us too softly he wouldn't have gained our respect and if he'd come in too hard we may have rebelled.

Senior Hanley treated Jacko's memory with deference but he

didn't let us dwell on the past. If anything, he drove us harder then Jacko had done but was fair in his comments and criticisms and helped those who needed it. His catch-phrase was 'There is more in you' meaning we could always do better if we pushed ourselves.

The religious thing worried us at the start. Most of us were heathens who believed the only higher power was the chief inspector.

Cadets from the other sections immediately named us the God Squad, in that sensitive way 18-year-old boys have. We followed suit and nicknamed Senior Hanley "The Godfather". He was chuffed, I think but he was so inscrutable it was hard to tell.

The tone of our lessons certainly changed. With Jacko every second word had been a swear word and almost every story made even the most worldly of us blush. Senior Hanley never swore in class or in his private life. In fact the only time he ever swore was when he was playing an offender in a practical exercise and boy, did he throw himself into the part! Jacko would have been proud of him. We reckoned playing the baddy was a cathartic release for him.

Senior Hanley didn't share Jacko's interest in the outdoors but that didn't worry us as our PT instructors were keeping us busy. We had started learning self-defence and the emphasis was shifting from fitness based activities to more practical skills.

Map-reading was first and I expected to excel. I had proven myself quite adept at finding my way home in all sorts of sorry states, so I was confident my sense of direction was better than average. I had even thought up an acronym for my homing instinct. I called it WASOD, the Wood Amazing Sense Of Direction. Plus, I'd crapped out at typing, pistol-shooting and spelling, so I was due a win. Yes indeedy, bring on the map reading exercises: I was ready.

When our instructors announced we were going on an orienteering exercise I almost scoffed. Orienteering, pah! Poncing around after little bits of paper over a few farmer's fields - piece of piss. Of course I'd forgotten where I was. When the police said orienteering what they actually meant was poncing around after little bits of paper while scaling treacherous cliffs, fording freezing flooded rivers, climbing mountains that goats took one look at and flagged away, and traversing foul-smelling boggy swamps.

The appointed day was bitterly cold and there was a howling gale. Our instructors thought the conditions perfect. My map kept blowing away, the lead in my pencil snapped, my boots filled with mud and small sharp stones and, just to be tricky, our instructors had purposefully given us the wrong coordinates for one of the locations. They wanted to see how long we would blunder about looking for something that obviously wasn't there. The answer was a bloody long time, and by the end of the day WASOD's credibility had taken a battering. We got back to the bus cold, wet, smelly, totally disheartened and completely knackered. Our instructors proclaimed the exercise a roaring success.

Other skill-based activities we undertook half way through the second term included wrestling, athletics, and baton and handcuff training.

We were disappointed when we finally got our batons as they turned out to be much smaller then we'd imagined. They had the same size and consistency as a large sausage, which made me wonder how much use they would be in an emergency. I didn't think offenders would tremble with fear when confronted by a policeman brandishing a wooden bratwurst. I doubted our new toys had much real offensive or defensive power. I was wrong. Those little pieces of wood could be very effective when used correctly. It came down to where you hit the person. Smack them in the forearm and it only served to enrage, but if you gave them a sharp rap on the elbow then you could take their whole arm out of play. The same high-pain factors applied to the fingers, the wrist, the shins, the kneecaps and the bridge of the nose, though the last one is normally reserved for Bruce Willis movies.

Handcuffs were another matter entirely. Simple to use and hours of fun for the whole family. We knew they'd be cool right from the start and we wasted no time practicing. They were made of really solid metal and once applied, the only way to release them was the owner's key, although there was a general-release key that all police officers carried.

This key came in very useful at Trentham as once the handcuffs had been issued there was an inevitable spate of cadet cuffing. Our instructors had pre-empted the arrival of our batons and handcuffs with a series of lectures on the correct application of said weapons and we were left in no doubt that improper use would lead to instant and terrible retribution. But, boys will be boys, and until the novelty wore off our handcuffs were used on a wide variety of things - family members, household pets, chair legs, steering wheels, girlfriends - in an equally wide variety of creative locations.

We had to be careful, when it came to applying the cuffs in jest. Put on too tightly and the handcuffs could cut off a person's circulation and cause severe pain. In police work this was often desirable, because if you've gone to the trouble of cuffing someone they must have either been very naughty or really annoyed you.

To make it easier to get the cuffs on a struggling offender, our instructor's taught us a nifty trick. If we pushed the arms of our handcuffs right up to the very last click on the ratchet, then bashed the cuffs against the offender's wrist, the force would push through the last click and the handcuffs would spin in a quick loop, snapping tightly around the wrist. This was not only extremely effective but it looked cool. The only problem was it was hard to judge where the final ratchet click was. If you set the handcuffs two or three clicks back from the end of the ratchet, not only would the cuffs fail to open when you hit them against the wrist, but it bloody hurt. This would have been fine if we had been practicing on offenders but as the only guinea pigs available were family members, friends or each other, it was less than ideal. Fortunately our minds were taken off handcuff and baton practice by the next activity our instructors had planned. Boxing.

They decided the best way to foster harmony in our section

was to have us beat the crap out of one another. I was looking forward to it. I fancied myself as a boxer. I'm pretty solid and can throw a good punch, the only problem being that my blows take a while to arrive; you could stop and read a newspaper and still not get caught with one. I don't just telegraph punches I send them by Morse code. Despite this glaring chink in my armour I was confident I'd do well.

The rules of the fights were simple. We were to stand toe to toe on a mat and hit each other until one or both fell over. Head protectors and boxing gloves were provided so it's not as bad as it could have been, but a solid blow to the head will still send your brain bouncing around your skull no matter how well encased it is. After a few weeks of practice we were ready for the 'real' fights.

Unsurprisingly, I had a reputation as a slow and predictable puncher, although it was acknowledged that if I did manage to catch you, it hurt.

Phil was one of the worst boxers in the section and he was also my best mate, so it seemed unfair when we were paired off to fight each other. I was much bigger than he was and should have been able to thump him easily. I had every intention of doing so, too - not through malice, but because it was what the exercise demanded and I was a competitive bastard.

For the first minute of the bout I caught Phil with a couple of heavy blows and things looked bad for him. Then the PT instructor began giving my opponent hints as we fought. I could hear him telling Phil to watch my boxing pattern. Every time I came forward I led with two left jabs then swung a big right hook. He told Phil to step outside the hook and hit me as I swung through. I could hear these instructions clearly but it never occurred to me to change my style. Duh! So in I went, left, left, big right, big miss, Phil clipped me behind the ear as I swung and the next thing I know I'm eating canvas. He hadn't hurt or dazed me but had caught me off balance and tipped me over. A huge cheer went up, as the underdog had won.

When we got back to the barracks a couple of the other cadets came into my room and had a predictable laugh at my expense. As they were leaving one said the fight had done Phil's confidence a world of good. Didn't do much for mine though.

Wrestling was a different story. I was brilliant, holding off four opponents at the same time and not being floored until they got five on me. Modesty forbids a blow-by-blow description; suffice to say I was possibly the best wrestler Trentham – nay, the world - has ever seen.

I found self-defence training fascinating. Amongst all the neat tricks we learned, we were also shown how to remove protesters from protest sites. This is actually really tricky because protesters normally employ a non-violent stance and it is much easier to throw someone in the paddy wagon if they are expending all their energy waving their arms about. If they just go all saggy and flop on the ground it is like moving a dead weight and can tie up a couple of officers. I suggested tickling them to get them moving them but my proposal was rather pointedly ignored by the instructors.

We were also taught effective ways to restrain violent people (several of which I've employed successfully to impress girls at parties) and a couple of dynamite throws.

One of the most impressive demonstrations occurred when we were being shown how to disarm a person with a knife. Instead of just showing us how to do it our P.T instructors (who could teach the Sadists Society a trick or two) set one cadet, armed with a wooden knife, against an unarmed one. The first couple of guys got stabbed in disturbingly quick and nasty fashions by their assailants, with one cadet showing worrying familiarity with a knife. He claimed it was due to many years in the catering industry but I have my doubts.

After mopping up the blood from the many mortally wounded Cadets lying moaning around the gymnasium the instructors got ready to send another lamb to the slaughter. This lamb, however, had had five years of tai kwon do experience behind him, and as the wolf with the knife approached he whipped into a spinning back kick and booted the weapon clean out of the other guy's hand. It was one of the most impressive things I've ever seen. I always thought martial arts were a load of old hokum, with little or no practical application, but after seeing that display I was converted. Not to the extent of actually learning any of the stuff (I still laugh heartily at a mate of mine who practices tai chi), but next time I attack someone with a knife I want written confirmation that he is not a deft exponent of kung fu.

To compensate for the regular beatings we were receiving in the gymnasium we were given more leave weekends and discipline wasn't quite so strict. Bookings were still handed out regularly but not with the gay abandon of the first term. One concession the instructors did grant us was we no longer had to march to meals. I was well pleased as I hated marching and lining up, especially as several of the cadets used the occasion to have a laugh at my expense.

I have a big nose. There, I've said it. I think it's in proportion to the rest of my body but there is no getting past the fact that from side on it's a whopper.

One favourite barrack's joke was that when I lay down I looked like a two car garage. Another claimed that I would always be able to tell the time if I lost my watch as all I had to do was lie on my back and use my nose as a sundial. Ha ha ha.

I was standing at the front of the queue one day when a cadet further down the line called my name. When I turned around the next six cadets in line ducked simultaneously as if to avoid being knocked over by my nose. Everyone found this most amusing. Almost as amusing as my continual efforts to perfect an incendiary device to devastate all opposition should the need arise.

I was still stinging from my public humiliation over the beer-can bazooka and felt I needed a pyrotechnical success to restore my credibility as an explosives expert. It was not to be. A series of projects went with a phut rather than a bang and the one device that did burst spectacularly into flames almost burnt the barracks down.

I had conducted the experiment in the rubbish tin in my room but the bomb exploded with such unexpected ferocity it caused a fire. The metal bin quickly got too hot to handle and the flames fierce enough to stop me getting close. Worst of all, the mat the bin was sitting on had started smoking. Fortunately Phil had the presence of mind to grab his bin and fill it full of water, dowsing the fire (and my mat) before the room went up. This was long before smoke detectors so my gross negligence wasn't immediately discovered. I was planning for it never to be, but there was the little detail of a soggy and burnt mat which we had to get past the people who used white gloves to detect dust particles in our room. Hiding a large burn mark in the rug that, according to regulations, had to sit conspicuously on the floor beside the bed, would be tricky. I wasn't sure but I seemed to remember arson being frowned upon by the constabulary. Losing the mat was my only option - but how? Phil had an idea. He suggested swapping it with his room-mate's mat. I loved the thought but, spaggot though the guy was; he wasn't dim enough not to notice a mat switch.

In the end I decided to stick roughly to the truth by confessing to a fire in my bin but revising how the fire started. Even this was fraught with difficulties as there was no smoking allowed in the barracks (I don't smoke anyway), so the careless cigarette butt excuse was out. In the end I went for a dubious tale of trying to melt two broken bits of plastic together with a match which wasn't out properly when I threw it in the bin. I received a booking for my actions, saved only from a stricter sentence because my Gonzo reputation gave my stupid story some credibility. It was one of the few times in my life that being an accident-prone jinx worked in my favour.

Our first leave weekend of the second term arrived with me on two bookings again but this time I threw caution to the wind and tried not to get a third. Much to my astonishment this daring plan worked and I took off really early on Saturday morning for Palmerston North. I arrived at 7am, the morning half gone for a police cadet, but still the middle of the night for a teachers' college student.

Blair Tennent was dark and silent. The only light shone from the Matron's window. I had to get in, Carey's willpower had been sorely tested by my last visit and I was hoping to breech her defences this weekend. Besides, I was bloody cold and wanted to get into her warm room to be fussed over and cuddled. In a tough policeman sort of way, of course.

The problem was getting in undetected. I needed help from the inside, preferably from Carey. I decided to use the tried and true method of throwing small stones at her window. But which window was hers? I knew the way to her room from the inside but from where I was standing all the rooms looked the same. There was nothing else for it so I picked a window and biffed a handful of stones at it. After all, what was the worst thing that could happen if I got the wrong room? I could frighten one of the girls, who could mistake me for a prowler and alert the Hell Matron who would ban me from Blair Tennent forever.

Fortunately this didn't happen. I did get the wrong room but my luck was in because the girl I awoke was a friend of Carey's and she recognised me. Before long I was smuggled inside and being cuddled unmercifully. Naturally I fought against it, but what's a guy to do?

The weekend was great, but the trip back to Trentham was a sorry saga. It was the first of many trips that ended with me trudging into a mate's room in the barracks and saying "That was the worst trip I have ever had."

This particular mate's name was Mark, he had a dry sense of humour and we got on well. His room was just down the hall from Aqua's and after several hell trips in Floyd, Aqua and Phil would wait in Mark's room for my return, so they'd be first to hear the latest tale of woe. Floyd had been immortalised by the 'falling-out window' incident, plus Jacko's highly exaggerated stories told after admitting he'd borrowed my car. Jacko decided the mileage he could get from colourful Death Mini tales far outweighed the shame of having borrowed Floyd in the first place. Good old Jacko.

There had also been a couple of ignition problems and one 'brakes failing and colliding with the barracks fence' occurrence that fuelled the legend. But the incident which did the most damage was an innocent drive around Trentham one Sunday afternoon. I'd enlisted Fozzie as passenger, hoping for a good report to counter all the bad ones. He was reluctant to set foot inside the mini, but being called a wuss in front of his peers changed his mind. Besides, it was becoming a status symbol to have travelled in Floyd and lived to tell the tale.

We had been driving around for about 20 minutes and Fozzie was just starting to relax, when we hit a pothole. Fozzie let out a terrified yell. 'Chill out!' I told him, it hadn't been much of a bump. He replied that it wasn't the bump so much as the fact that the floor had fallen out of the car.

Yeah, sure. I glanced over to see the passenger-side floor had indeed disappeared, giving Fozzie a fine view of the road rushing by, but no-where to put his feet. This was hard to come back from, so I laughed pathetically and told him with some Minis the floor was optional.

He demanded I take him back to the barracks immediately and wasted no time blabbing to anyone who would listen (the entire cadet force and most of the instructors). Needless to say, my every journey was now eagerly awaited, especially the long ones to Palmerston North.

I had the floor fixed at a local garage before my next trip to see Carey. The mechanic was reluctant to have anything to do with the car but money changed his mind and he welded a solid plate onto the passenger-side floor. When he had finished, he clonked it with a large spanner and proclaimed that nothing was going to get through that sucker. How right he was.

I returned to Trentham on a wet and windy Sunday night. It had been pouring all day and there were big puddles of water all over the place. This didn't slow me down as much as it should have because I was in a hurry to get back before curfew. About halfway through my journey I noticed a 'Flooding Ahead' sign on the brow of a hill. I ignored it and carried on down the other side until I saw a mass of water before me. 'Right,' I thought, 'the best thing to do here is accelerate.'

I should probably mention that I don't have the greatest driving history. I failed my licence the first two times and only passed the test a week before I got into Trentham. Dad had given up trying to teach me after I drove into the side of the house while practicing reversing in the back of our section. He said he could have understood me finding the width of the vehicle hard to judge if I'd been driving his Falcon 500, but as I was in Mum's Hillman Elf, one of the smallest cars in the world, it was beyond him. In the end he paid for me to have driving lessons and I finally managed to squeak through the test.

Anyway, my six months of driving experience told me that planting boot was the right thing to do when approaching a small lake in a lightweight Mini, in pitch-black, wet conditions. As soon as I hit the water I began reassessing my plan but by then it was too late. A huge gush of water exploded through the gear stick, absolutely soaking me and flooding the interior. This was the least of my worries as the steering wheel had been wrenched out of my hands and the car had spun around 180 degrees, literally floating. As I wiped water from my eyes I was surprised to see I was now facing the way I had just come, on the wrong side of the road, in a stalled, waterlogged car.

My brain, tuned to react in milliseconds in a crisis, immediately assessed the situation and told me something was wrong. Taking this on board, I leapt from the car and pushed/floated Floyd to a less death-inducing part of the road. I was bloody lucky there was no traffic. I was also extremely fortunate that Floyd spun around on roughly the same spot and didn't careen off the road or into a bank.

Once my heart had made its way back from my mouth to its rightful place in my chest I took a look at the damage. On the plus side Floyd was very clean. Conversely we were both dripping wet and there was 30 centimetres of water sloshing around on the newly welded floor, now sealed tighter than a vacuum-packed condom. It took half an hour for Floyd's electrics to dry out and then, by some miracle, he started and I drove, very carefully back to Trentham. I'd bailed out some of the water but there was still a small river sloshing around every time I turned a corner. I arrived at Trentham just before lights out, slumped down on a chair in Mark's room and said "That was the worst trip I have ever had."

GASSED

Later that week I was sent to a mental institution. As part of our studies on mental health we were required to spend time doing community service at public medical facilities around the Wellington area. Some cadets spent a week at the accident and emergency wards; I got the loony bin.

This was familiar ground for me as Mum and Dad had been heavily involved with the Intellectually Handicapped Society for many years. My younger brother was handicapped at birth when the umbilical cord wrapped around his neck and cut off oxygen to his brain. He was so seriously disabled that he had to be institutionalised for life. After this, Mum started working with intellectually handicapped people and has been helping them ever since. My brother died at the age of 17 and though we visited him at least twice a year he never showed any signs that he recognised us.

My background should have prepared me for the experience but it didn't. The people Mum and Dad dealt with usually suffered from Downs Syndrome or were of below-average intelligence. Few were dangerous. They were more like big kids - quite loving but incapable of looking after themselves. Most were quite happy, not really able to comprehend life being any different.

The people in the secure unit at the institution I visited were completely different. At first sight they looked normal enough but after spending some time with them I discovered they were definitely playing scrabble without any vowels.

I spent a few days with the male patients first and was taken into the secure unit. And very secure it was. I had to go through three solidly locked doors to get into the area where the patients were. By the second door I was beginning to have grave reservations about this particular assignment and was ready to do a runner. But, it was too late.

I found myself in a spacious room with a sunny glass frontage that looked over a small park. It seemed quite restful. This was the day room, where the patients would come and read books or play table tennis or watch television. Several large orderlies in white coats walked around the room and kept an eye on things. I was told to sit in a chair and observe what was going on. The patients had been told I was a police cadet and was visiting the facility as part of my training. They looked quite impressed for a few minutes and then ignored me completely. I sat in a chair at the back of the room and watched a couple of guys playing table tennis. After 10 minutes a young, perfectly sane looking bloke came and sat next to me.

"Hello," he said.

"Hello," I replied.

"I'm here on assignment too," he said.

"Oh," said I, relieved to find a kindred spirit. "What are you studying?"

"I'm not studying anything," he whispered conspiratorially. "I'm a spy."

"Oh shit," I thought, then I said. "That's nice."

At this point I wished he would go away but no, he insisted on telling me all his spying plans. I mentioned I didn't think it was very good spy procedure to tell me all his secret stuff but was informed he'd been lying anyway so it didn't really matter. He wasn't a spy after all; he was an undercover Policeman.

I tried desperately to catch the eye of one of the orderlies but they seemed to be looking the other way with strange smiles on their faces.

My new friend, the undercover policeman, was in the middle of a fascinating story about a drugs bust that went wrong when he suddenly stood up and pointed at me, screaming "You've blown my cover!" Then before I could say anything he turned around and ran flat out at the plate-glass window.

It all happened in slow motion. I was standing now, watching in horror and yelling to the orderlies, one of whom turned but didn't react quickly enough. The maniac (medical term) hit the glass with a sickening thud, then, to my amazement, bounced back into the room and fell on the floor. A couple of orderlies picked him up and carted him off to his room. As I stood there, mouth agape, another orderly came over and led me to the huge window. He tapped the glass, grinned, and told me it was reinforced safety glass, practically unbreakable. Apparently my spy/policemen friend wasn't the first inmate to try and smash through it.

'They do that occasionally, said the orderly, as if describing someone sipping tea from the wrong side of the cup. I didn't know what to say so I said nothing and retreated to my chair then tried to make myself as inconspicuous as possible.

The next person to strike up a conversation with me was a guy in his mid fifties. He was a very polite and gentle man who had a fascination for Alsatian dogs. Being a dog lover myself I enjoyed my chat with him and when he asked if I'd like to see his collection of dog sketches I said I'd love too. The orderlies gave me permission to go to his room to look at his paintings, as long as a doctor went with us. I thought they were being over-cautious - he was a harmless old coot, a bit of a talker but actually quite shy.

His pencil drawings were amazing. This guy could really draw. He had several beautiful pictures of German Shepherds and had done some very nice water colours as well. Once he had shown me his collection he thanked me for my interest and bid me good day as he was getting tired and wanted a rest. When we had left his room the doctor asked me to follow him. He took me into his office and showed me the old guy's file.

Six months ago my friend the Alsatian-lover had been walking down a main street in Wellington when a voice in his head told him the man across the street was laughing at him. He picked up a vegetable knife from a stall in a fruit shop, crossed the road and stabbed the innocent man in the throat, killing him instantly.

I felt physically sick when I read his file: it was full of madness and delusion. To me he had seemed like someone's sad old grandad. It scared me to think that I hadn't even an inkling that something was terribly wrong with him. The doctor made me feel better by telling me his patient was completely normal 90 per cent of the time, and then he'd become delusional and snap. I'd heard about people like this but had never met one. It had been a truly frightening day.

The next day was worse. I was off to the women's top security unit. One of the doctors told me the women patients were generally more dangerous than the men because they were less predictable. I hadn't noticed a lot of predictability in the men so could hardly wait to see the girls. I'd only been in the secure unit for 2 minutes when one of the women came up to me and said, 'I'm a snake - do you like my scales?'

Being the well bought-up guy I am, I replied that I thought her scales were lovely. This can't have been the right answer because she hissed at me and slithered away.

Shortly after this initiation I witnessed one of the snake's friends attack the female orderlies. The patient was standing quietly in the corner one minute then the next thing I knew she was screaming like a banshee and attacking anyone in her immediate vicinity. She was quickly grabbed by the orderlies and I was asked to help get her into a secure room. The woman was still howling and screaming and even though her arms were pinned she was kicking and biting like she was possessed (maybe she was). When we got her to the examination room, I, for one, was exhausted. She had fought us every inch of the way and hadn't calmed down until we pinned her to the bed. One of the nurses decided the patient should be sedated. She went away and returned a few minutes later with a large syringe on a tray. As she approached the bed I felt the patient relax, so I loosened my hold on her. It was a rookie mistake because, quick as a flash, she jerked herself out of my grip, grabbed the syringe and swung the needle at my forehead. I moved back just in time to avoid getting a hypodermic in the eye. Fortunately, one of the orderlies had managed to get a hand on her swinging arm, which had slowed her down.

I grabbed the crazy woman's wrist and twisted the syringe away from her. She screamed with frustration. For a small woman she was incredibly strong and it took all my strength to get the needle out of her hand. I gave the syringe to the nurse, who wasted no time in sticking it into the patient's arm. About five minutes later the woman had calmed down and was lying strapped to the bed with a glazed look in her eyes.

I apologised straight away to the nurse for relaxing my grip and she was very nice about it, saying it was a trick the patients often used. They would lull you into a false sense of security and then they'd strike. She said you got used to it after a while. Not me, I thought: I had no intention of staying in that place one millisecond longer than I had to.

The rest of the day passed without any more violent outbursts, (unless you count my own after one of the nurses beat me at pool during lunch hour) but it was impossible to relax in the secure unit. The patients watched you like psychotic hawks, just waiting for you to show a signs of weakness they could exploit. A bit like our instructors back in Trentham, come to think of it.

The next couple of days were spent with the out-patients,

voluntary patients who hadn't been placed under protective care. Some seemed to be just as dangerous as the incarcerated ones, the only difference being they had yet to commit a crime, or be caught committing a crime.

I saw a lot of genuinely sad cases as well. People whose lives had been ruined through depression, and sane, rational folk, who had just been worn down by day-to-day life. I can't say I enjoyed community service at the mental institution, but I certainly learnt a lot.

Next up was driving school. I was dreading this. I had already proved my abilities behind the wheel needed work so why drag me through the humiliation of cocking it up in public?

A and B section had already done driving school and by all accounts it was really hard. Wayne had caused a sensation by being the first cadet in the wing to have a smash. He hit a bus - or claimed the bus hit him. I found highly amusing. If you remember, Wayne was the extremely tidy one, and his driving was just like his housekeeping, methodical and error-free.

It was one of life's great ironies that Mr Perfect was the only cadet to have a crash, and one I milked for all it was worth. I wasn't the only one either. Wayne got a new nickname - TY - after the code number on the form a police officer has to fill out when he damages a car on duty. His smash also took the heat off my anticipated disasters, for a while anyway.

The driving instructors were even more sadistic and sarcastic than our other instructors, unbelievable as that may seem. My first time driving with one of these guys was an extremely nerve-racking experience, especially after they discovered I'd only had my driver's license for six months. They treated me like a complete novice, showing me where to put the key and which way to turn it (I had some ideas on where I would like to have stuck the key but kept them to myself.)

It started spitting with rain halfway through my first drive and after 5 minutes I noticed my instructor had moved very close to the windscreen and was peering out of it. I took the hint and activated the windscreen wipers. As the blade passed in front of his face my instructor suddenly leapt back yelling, 'The road! The road! There it is!' Sarcastic bastard.

That set the tone for the rest of driving school - even the section's most experienced drivers were getting a hard time. Our every move was scrutinised and our every mistake leapt upon.

Despite the barbs and the pressure, we learned a lot. The practical exercises were cool, too. We did a number of interesting driving exercises and reflex tests. One in particular involved a large set of traffic lights and three lanes made out of cones. Instead of having red, orange and green colours in the traffic lights there was an arrow pointing left, an arrow pointing right and the word 'stop' lit up in red. The exercise required us to drive towards the lights at a set speed, then react according to which light came on. The instructors delayed illuminating the light until the last possible second. If we went the wrong way or knocked over a cone the instructor tutted and wrote in his book in red ink.

The three speeds we had to travel at were 30 kilometres an hour, 50 kilometres an hour and 80 kilometres an hour. At 30 I got a left-hand arrow and made it into the lane, knocking over two cones as I turned (a shake of the head and a tut). At 50 I anticipated a right arrow or a stop but got a left arrow and drove into the wrong lane, knocking over two cones (a head shake and the red pen). At 80 they illuminated the stop sign but I didn't react quickly enough, locked up the brakes and skidded, annihilating five cones and a sand bag (a shake of the head, two tuts and the red pen). Worse was to come.

Our next driving test was held at Manfield racetrack which had been hired for the day. Not content with sending novices onto a professional racing circuit, our driving instructors made the track harder by putting cones around the course. They used them to cut down the angles on the corners and placed two cones close together in the middle of the back straight, expecting us to drive between them at top speed without knocking them over. A generous 12 centimetres had been allowed on either side. At the end of the straight was a vicious right-hander, leading into a series of S-bends. To make the hairpin corner even tougher they placed cones on the front right of the bend, narrowing the angle and making the course's most difficult corner virtually impossible.

One unexpected bonus occurred when we went driving at Manfield. Carey was able to sneak away from teachers' college for the day and she and two friends joined us at the track. Manfield is located near Palmerston North and it seemed a shame to be so close

147

but yet so far. Naturally I had asked permission for the girls to come along but never dreamt it would actually be granted. It seemed the driving school instructors liked the idea of having a female audience and approval was granted. I decided to take full advantage of having my girl at the track and sauntered over to Carey, gave her a hug and asked the girls to join us at the starting blocks. As I was the only cadet with any female company, my standing in the male ranks went up considerably. Not for long, as it turned out, but for now I was riding high. I had bought not one, but three girls to Manfield for my female-obsessed colleagues to ogle. I was pretty damn cool.

The instructors thought themselves cooler and asked the girls if they'd like to go for a ride around the track with 'real' police drivers after we 'pretend' cops had finished. The girls replied coyly that it would be fun and it was all arranged. This sounded dodgy to me but the glimmer of a driving school pass convinced me to keep my mouth shut. Having finished flirting with my girlfriend and her mates (for the time being), our driving school instructors turned their attention back to us.

We were told to do three laps of the circuit as fast as we could without knocking over any of the cones. Our instructors would be watching us from the control room and would be in touch via the car RT to correct any problems we were having. We drove in alphabetical order and by the time they got to me everyone but Phil had driven. Nearly every driver had knocked over cones but no-one had done much wrong.

I got through my first lap with no problems at all, even

managing to boot it between the cones on the straight without tipping them. The second lap went well too with the instructor saying I was doing okay but that I should brake before the corners rather than into them. 'Yeah, yeah,' I thought, now completely in control of the vehicle and ready to push it harder in the last lap. The male urge to show off in front of his mate had kicked in and I decided to really go for it. I was confident I could handle both the vehicle and the track. I reckon this weakness in the male psyche has caused more problems than both politics and religion put together.

Add this to a recurring problem I've had in my life - I get something right, I become overconfident and I push it too far – and you have a truly lethal combination. (I still do this by the way. You would have thought that after 50 years of injury and accident I would have learned something). At Manfield, I'd only had 18 years of injury and accident behind me and knew nothing.

I hit the straight at full throttle, cleared the two cones (one wobbling slightly) and approached the tight right-hander, still going flat out. This time I thought I'd feather the brakes in the corner and accelerate out of it. Imagine my surprise when the car left the track and began spinning round and round in the grass. Suddenly I was facing the wrong way on the grass verge, which luckily was quite large.

The engine had stalled and the only sound I could hear was laughter coming out of the RT. Then I received a message from my instructor: 'Gonzo, you're supposed to drive on the other side of the cones.'

I started the car, reversed off the grass and limped cautiously through the s-bends to the finishing post. Phil came and took the keys, saying nothing but giving me a look of immense sympathy. I was the only cadet out of the entire wing to spin out at Manfield, a fact that every cadet found highly amusing and, as you can imagine, it frequently cropped up in conversation.

Carey was, of course, hugely supportive, saying she was very impressed at the way I managed to get the car out of the grass without hitting anything else.

The grins on the faces of her mates were removed soon after. It was time for the instructors to show off their driving skills. Well, one of the instructors anyway. Their chief was an extremely experienced police driver who had done a considerable amount of motor sport racing as well. He was the one who volunteered to give the girls a quick spin around the track. I don't think Carey and her friends had taken the offer seriously but there was no way they could get out of it now. They hopped nervously into the car, Carey in the front and the other two in the back, then off they went.

Man, that guy could drive. He burnt rubber at the start, hung the car into the corners and gunned it down the straight without looking even slightly out of control. I caught a glance of the girls as he completed the first lap and had to smile at the panic in their eyes. From trackside the instructor's driving was bloody impressive; apparently from inside the car it had been terrifying. The girls exited the vehicle white as sheets; all claiming never to have been so scared in their entire lives. The instructor was very pleased with himself.

And somehow, next time I saw the girls, I got it in the neck for getting them into such a death-defying situation. I spluttered my innocence but to no avail.

Only a third of the cadets passed driving school. I wasn't among them. We were assessed on every aspect of driving, with marks ranging from poor to excellent. Only three excellents were awarded and, in a moment of supreme irony, I received one of them. It was awarded for my outstanding ability in crossing railway lines. The rest of my marks were poor or average. This meant I wasn't allowed to drive a police car anywhere other than at railway crossings. I suspect someone was taking the piss.

We were told later that a high failure rate was normal and those of us who failed would re-sit their police license at our station of placement. A license would be issued if we passed the station test, which apparently involved driving around the block without hitting anyone.

Having just sent us to the loony bin and given us every opportunity to wipe ourselves out in speeding vehicles, our instructors decided it was time to blow us up.

Yes, explosives were next, as you can imagine, I was very excited. Perhaps now I could discover where I'd gone wrong with the beer-can bazooka and my home-made incendiary devices.

Before we were told how to make things go bang, we received a stern lecture on the dangers of explosives. We were warned about the severe consequences of playing around with ammunition of any kind. As if.

I did notice Senior Sergeant Hanley shooting a few looks my way during the lecture - I could only assume he was lining me up as an unofficial leader for the upcoming demonstrations. The more inexperienced cadets would be able to come to me for advice and guidance. Inexplicably, he forgot to spell this out, but still, we were going to blow things up so I got over my disappointment quickly.

Because the police are not as good as the army at demolishing things, our instructors brought in armed forces explosives experts to show us what to do. In my opinion 'bomb-blower-upperers' are gods, so when I first saw the army guys I felt let down. These so-called explosive 'experts' had little or no visible scarring and had all their fingers. Surely any bombardier worth his salt would have used too much jelly at some point or stood too close to the blast area. I mean, you are supposed to learn by your mistakes so, in an area like explosives, you'd expect visible collateral damage. I was not an expert and I had inflicted multiple injuries to my person, so it stood to reason that a real pro would be sans limbs. These soldiers were way too unscathed to be real bomb guys.

Surprisingly, they seemed to know their stuff. They told us about cordite and detonators and time switches and black powder and fuses and dynamite. They even told us what to watch out for if we received a bomb call. They were less forthcoming with actual disarming information. In fact, when I asked them which wire I should cut when faced with a ticking bomb, they said that I shouldn't be cutting anything and should be calling the bomb squad instead. Undeterred, I suggested the credible scenario of the bomb squad van crashing on its way to the site and there only being 2 minutes left in which to defuse the device and save the city. They told me if this happened I should use the eenie, meenie, minee, moe method.

The lectures were cool and I was dying to get on with the actual blowing up stuff, which we'd be doing the next day. We were driven out to the army bomb site early the next morning and were told to line up around a roped-off area. Inside the ropes were all sorts of exciting things, all primed to be blown to smithereens.

The demonstrations got under way immediately. First were the small bangs as we were shown how detonators worked. I was amazed at the power of these tiny explosive devices - they did enough damage by themselves so it was scary to think what they could do when attached to a decent-sized bomb.

Next we were shown the blast from a single stick of dynamite (big and loud), then a coil of cordex was bought out. The cordex rope looked like an ordinary wire but was highly explosive. As we were having its properties explained, the world's stupidest duck flapped down from the sky and sat on the wire. The instructor, literally seconds away from detonation, wondered why his audience had suddenly burst out laughing. The hilarity was followed by cruel but funny cries of 'blow up the duck!' The instructor took pity on the dumb creature and shooed it away. Once the duck was safely clear he pushed the detonator. The cordex rope went up with a bright flash and a kurrump noise. It was most impressive. That duck never knew just how close he came to becoming an entree.

After the explosion our instructor proved he was less sympathetic to humans. He told us if you wrapped a strand of the cordex around someone's neck then detonated it, it would blow the head clean off the body. Then he cackled. I wasn't alone in finding this a little scary.

The blasts got bigger and louder as a fascinating array of explosives were detonated. We were hoping the grand finale would be a car being blown up, as we'd been told that had happened the year before, but it was not to be. They'd detonated one a few weeks earlier and a soldier had been injured by a flying tyre. This made them gun shy, so to speak. Instead they'd dug a 10-metre hole in the ground, packed it with high explosives and then filled it with water.

We were moved around to the far side of the rope and told to watch the hole.

So intent were we on not missing the blast that we failed to notice our instructors sneaking off to the other side of the rope. The miserable sods were planning to soak us with the lake of water that was about to be blasted into the air.

That day fate was on the side of the cadets: the wind changed just before the explosives were detonated. There was a huge boom and the ground beneath our feet shook. A single column of water blew straight up in the air to a height of about 10 metres, then, to our great delight, cascaded down upon our instructors.

They had their revenge later in the day during an Armed Offenders

Squad demonstration. We were shown a number of tactics used by the AOS, which I found very interesting given my recent experience as an armed offender. The squad worked brilliantly as a team and were very skilled. It made me realise how well I'd done to have shot a couple of AOS members during the exercise in New Plymouth. These guys really knew their stuff. They moved like ghosts and if you were lucky enough to see them moving then they also had you in their gun sights.

After going through a few basic manoeuvres they familiarised us with their weaponry. Most impressive it was, too, and we had live demonstrations for the rest of the afternoon. Towards the end of the day they brought out the smoke grenades then showed us how to explode them and use the smoke as cover. Next came the highlight of the demonstration, tear gas.

There are several types of tear gas bombs. The one we were shown looks like a rocket and is fired from a bazooka-style gun. It is an effective weapon for many reasons. Earlier in the year an offender had holed up in a caravan which was sitting in a large field. He had a rifle with him, making approaching the caravan very dangerous. The decision was made to fire a tear gas canister through the caravan window. The rocket style was selected as it flew further and straighter than the others because of three fins that flicked out the back when it was fired. The high-powered rocket ploughed straight through the side of the caravan into the interior. Seconds after the impact, and before the gas had a chance to disperse, the offender came flying out the door surrendered. He was in quite a state as he thought the tear gas canister was a mortar bomb and believed the police were trying to blow him up. Having seen the rocket (I nicked an empty one as a souvenir), I can understand his reaction. It really did look like a surface-to-air missile and it hasn't been in the police's interest to correct this misconception.

When asked if we'd like to see a practical tear gas demonstration we foolishly said yes and were told to stand in the middle of a nearby paddock. Our instructors said that we needed to be well clear of the firing zone so none of the gas would drift back towards us. This was a lie. We were the firing zone.

After we'd been standing in the field for a few minutes we heard a gentle thud and a canister flew over our heads to land behind us. This was followed by another canister to the left, one to the right and another in front. As huge clouds of gas billowed around us it didn't take a genius to work out we'd been deceived.

There was nowhere to run, and before long we were surrounded by tear gas. I foolishly decided the best thing to do would be to hold my ground. The gas couldn't be that bad and my best course of action would be to hold my breath and guts it out.

I was in the middle of the group and the cadets on the outside had already been hit by the fumes. I could hear coughing and spluttering but couldn't see them as the cloud closed in on me. By the time I was engulfed the field was full of cadets running like buggery through the mist, trying to get the hell out of there. It was eerie - bodies were everywhere, with some cadets crawling on the ground and others doubled over retching.

Seconds after the gas hit me I realised the folly of my plan. There was no way I could tough it out. The effects of the gas were brutal and instant: it burnt into my eyes and clawed its way down my throat, reacting violently to any moist part of the body. I ran as fast as I could to get out of the deadly cloud, then fell to my knees coughing, with my throat on fire and my eyeballs exploding.

When the mist lifted the field was littered with cadets rolling desperately on the ground trying to get the irritating burn off their skin.

Once our instructors finished having a good old chuckle they advised us not to shower when we got back to the barracks as the water would set the irritant off again. They weren't kidding - even several hours later the stuff still burned like hell and at shower time that night Trentham was alive with the sound of cadets moaning in pain. The day that started with a bang and ended with a whimper.

THE DEMON ALCOHOL: PART TWO

It was time for our second-term exams. During the term we had studied police powers of arrest, crimes involving dishonesty, serious crime, the Sale of Liquor Act and police computer use and procedures. I was reasonably confident I'd pass but dreading the three-day wait for results.

To stop us worrying about how we'd done our PT instructors had kindly scheduled a marathon. We were going to be running 42.2 kilometres the day before our results came out and two days before we were due to go on leave.

This didn't please me. I was fit enough to be able to do the marathon (just), but would be completely knackered and I wanted to conserve my energy for more pleasurable activities in Palmerston North. Like walks in the park and feeding the ducks. I also didn't want to risk getting a nasty groin strain before I arrived (after was okay).

There was only one thing for it: I was going to have to cheat. I mentioned my plan to Phil, who had also expressed concern over the marathon. He had a ski trip planned during his leave and wanted to get home uninjured.

Skiving off wasn't going to be easy, as our instructors had

timed the marathon beautifully. We couldn't pull a sickie because we had to be 100 per cent for our practical exams the day before the run, and taking a shortcut would be impossible as we were running through Whitman's Valley, which was too steep to bypass. There would also be a PT instructor standing at the 25km mark counting cadets as they staggered past.

Phil and I decided our best course of action would be to do the first 25 kilometres, then fake an injury that somehow involved both of us. A paper-thin plot, I'll admit, but it was all we had.

I was stuffed after 25 kilometres, though secretly quite pleased to have got that far. Phil was faring better as he was fitter than I was, and was having second thoughts about our plan. I didn't want to cheat alone but I could see his point. Both of us crapping out at the same time would look suspicious.

My legs were starting to ache and I desperately wanted to be in tip-top shape for the duck feeding. I had to stop so I pointed to a nearby bush and suggested we pop in there for a breather. Phil agreed, and as we were catching our breath I peeped out to see if I could spot any instructors lurking around. Instead I saw an old ute driving up the road. I came up with an instant plan and leapt from the bush sticking my thumb out in the universal signal of the hitch hiker.

To my amazement the ute stopped. A young guy was at the wheel and he agreed to give Phil and I a lift back to Trentham. Brilliant! He had seen the other runners so knew what we were up to and thought it was a great lark. He even chucked a blanket in the back so we could hide under it in case our instructors were using spotter helicopters (I wouldn't have put it past them).

Phil was reluctant at first but the skifields were beckoning so he agreed and we hopped into the back of the ute. The best part of the trip was sticking our heads over the edge of the tray and waving at the other cadets. They were struggling manfully onwards trying to complete the marathon in the conventional way and the looks on their faces were something I'll remember for ages.

Finally a plan was working - about bloody time. We were sure none of the other cadets would dob us in, as this form of cheating was highly acceptable - even admirable - if you had the balls to do it. Being caught in the back of the ute by an instructor wouldn't have been pretty though, and several weeks confinement to barracks would be the least we could expect.

The driver dropped us off at the gates of Trentham and we sneaked round the back of the gymnasium and hid. A trickle of cadets were coming past, heading for the finish line in the main compound. We couldn't join in yet as completing the race at the top of the field would have been laughable given the condition we were in at the 25km mark. A respectable time to appear would be near the end of the main bunch and we had a lovely rest waiting for the poor saps who had actually run the 42.2 kilometres to wobble past.

We popped out amongst a group of 8 totally knackered cadets and, despite some uncalled-for-comments about our parentage, joined them for the final jog to the finish line. The plan was an unqualified success and Phil and I came out of it fit and injury free.

Exam results came out the next day. I hadn't shone but had passed so I was happy. Two cadets weren't. They had failed for the second time and were told not to come back after leave. A bitter pill to swallow after eight months of training.

The next day I headed for Palmerston North. Quentin was with me as he'd been visiting friends in Wellington and had hit me up for a ride. On the straight outside Foxton I saw my chance to show Quentin what Floyd could do and planted boot getting the mini up to somewhere near the legal speed limit. Ahead of us in the distance a small old car driven by a small old man, pulled up to a stop sign at a side road. Ignoring the stop sign and us he began to creep forward. Quentin and I looked at each other in amazement and shook our heads in disbelief. He was pulling out right in front of us and we were in a pink mini. He must have been blind as a bat.

Still he carried on, creeping inexorably towards the middle of the road. It finally dawned on me that I would have to take evasive action to avoid the dangerous old duffer (Quentin yelling "We're going to die" helped my decision).

I slammed on the brakes, yanked on the hand brake and spun 360 degrees into the side street. As we skidded to a stop I wiped my brow and turned to Quentin to get his congratulations on what had been a spectacular piece of evasive driving. He wasn't there. He was lying in the middle of the road. Floyd's door had come open and he'd fallen out. Quentin was quite annoyed about this. Fortunately he wasn't injured aside from a few bumps and bruises.

As I got out to help him, the old twit in the old car crawled past and had the nerve to shake his head and tut-tut at us. I was gobsmacked: if I hadn't been so busy scraping Quentin off the road I would have chased him down and made a citizen's arrest.

Quentin was reluctant to get back in Floyd (big wuss) and it wasn't until I agreed to tie his door shut that he deigned to complete the journey. We reached Palmerston North without any further incidents but that was the last time Quentin ever travelled in Floyd.

Ahhhh, two weeks of leave. Two weeks of sleeping in, two weeks of making love to Carey (finally) and two weeks of explaining to my parents why I wasn't coming home. At least I had parents who were disappointed they wouldn't be seeing me: one cadet arrived home for leave to find that his parents had shifted without telling him.

I managed to stay out of trouble right up until the second-to-last night of my week of leave. It was a Friday night and Carey had a college function so I wouldn't be seeing her until later that evening. We were sitting around at Quentin's flat having a few beers when Quentin said he would like to try on my uniform. I didn't think it would fit him but let him have a go anyway. It was a bit baggy but looked okay.

Then he said how much fun it would be to act like a cop for an hour or so. The alarm bells should have started ringing but, sadly, they didn't. Quentin put an interesting scenario to me. How about he and I put on my uniform (me in pants, shirt and hat, he in civvy pants and police tunic), then we take a drive in his flatmate's car and bust some people. I told him this was not only highly illegal but it was also really dumb and dangerous.

'Hang on,' he cried, 'What if the people we arrested were friends of ours and we were only pretending - that wouldn't be against the law would it?'

It probably was but I was intrigued. Quentin suggested sending some of our friends to Pork Chop Hill (a local scenic lookout overlooking Palmerston North where teenager's went to ignore the view). Once they were in place we'd come roaring up in his flatmate's car, pretend to bust them, they'd escape, and we'd chase them back to the flat. It was the stupidest, most dumb-assed scheme I'd ever heard, I loved it.

Quentin made a few phone calls and the deal was on. His girlfriend even had a dodgy spinning orange light she'd 'borrowed' from some road works. We could put on the roof of the car (a 1970 Datsun 120Y) my friend suggested enthusiastically.

I can't think of a single reason why I even entertained this whole crazy deal. If we were caught it would be the end of my police career and Quentin and I risked being arrested for impersonating police officers. Somehow none of this occurred to me and I agreed to the plan. This highlighted my biggest problem at 18: the inability to think about the consequences of my actions.

Two car loads of friends drove up to Pork Chop Hill, which was full of necking teenagers. We arrived 10 minutes later. It was a spectacular entrance. Quentin was hanging out the passenger-side window of the car trying to hold the orange light on the roof. The batteries kept falling out so the light only worked in bursts.

How we could have thought anyone would believe the rusty old red Datsun with the weakly pulsing orange light, was an undercover police car I'll never know. Then there was Quentin's blatantly ill-fitting uniform and my epaulettes with CADET written on them in big white letters.

Still, there we were, skidding to a stop in the middle of the car park. We leapt out of the car and shone torches into other vehicles trying to look official. Surprisingly, all the onlookers bought it, hook, line and sinker.

It's amazing the power a police uniform (or bits of one) can have on the general public. Not one of these kids thought to question our authority, despite overwhelming evidence to the contrary. They happily let us write their names and addresses in our notebooks and when our friends roared off down the hill, they watched in awe as Quentin and I dived back into the Datsun and drove off in hot pursuit, orange light spluttering on the roof.

We got back to the flat high on adrenalin and laughter. Our friends were buzzing too. We'd played a grown-up game of cops and robbers and got away with it. They thought it was a great lark, which it had been, but I should have known better.

When I told Carey she hit the roof. She reminded me that in about six months' time I'd be arresting people who pulled stupid stunts like that. She couldn't believe how foolish I'd been, to risk everything I'd worked so hard for. I lamely tried to blame Quentin. I'd never seen Carey so angry before and it bought home the immaturity of my actions. It took a lot of grovelling and soul-searching before she'd even talk to me again. The lesson I learned that night would be with me right up until I did my next unbelievably idiotic thing, which was about two weeks away.

I went back to Trentham for our third and final term feeling sorry for myself. Carey's farewell had been decidedly frosty and I knew I had ground to make up on the romantic front.

It would be easier in the third term as we were allowed to apply for leave most weekends. Discipline was relaxed as well, with very few bookings dished out and more freedom allowed. We were told we'd have to do something really stupid, or fail our last exams badly, to get kicked out now. This was a relief but we still had a lot to learn and as always our fitness and stamina were constantly tested.

Our fourth RFL was scheduled for three days after the start of term and I made sure that I didn't accept any cans of Coke beforehand.

I felt really good on the RFL, posting my best results to date. I was fit, I was happy, and I'd penned some brilliant love letters to Carey and managed to repair the damage somewhat.

I received mail from my girlfriend with a regularity that astounded the other cadets. I was always at the front of the queue at mail-call time and a day rarely went past when I didn't get a letter. It was one of the many things the other cadets teased me about.

The ribbing was almost always in good fun but it did get

tiresome after a while. Particularly when it came to my taste in music. I was (and still am) a musical snob and my tastes sit on the fringes. The current week had been an exciting one for me as I'd discovered that legendary Irish blues guitarist Rory Gallagher was playing at the Wellington town hall that coming weekend. Naturally I thought interest amongst the cadets would be high and before class began I made an announcement to see who wanted to go with me. I was met by a stunned silence and then Fozzie spoke up: 'Why would we want to go and see some guy bend spoons.'

It took me a while to figure out what he was talking about; suddenly I clicked on.

'No, no, no,' I belatedly replied 'Not Uri Geller, Rory Gallagher.'

But it was too late. Everyone found it much funnier to think I was going to see an Irish spoon-bender and I got teased about it for the rest of the year. As a consequence no one would go to the concert with me so I went by myself. It was the loudest concert I've ever been to and I spent the next two days totally deaf. He was a bloody good guitarist though, and I'd like to say for the record he didn't bend one spoon all evening. Peasants.

The following Monday we were told we'd be spending the coming weekend on a marae in Hastings. I was still deaf from the concert and asked Phil who Marie from Hastings was, remarking that she must be a friendly girl to let 73 cadets stay with her. He cuffed me around the ear and yelled that we were staying on a Maori marae.

I got it then and prepared myself for a week of politically correct lectures from the general studies crew. They did not disappoint. I was a little nonplussed about the whole thing. Being from Taranaki I had been around Maori's all my life and never had a problem with the whole black and white thing. I'm not saying I was an exceptionally well adjusted, culturally sensitive sort of guy. If anything I'd avoided racism through apathy - I had no knowledge of what went on in other cultures and had no interest in finding out.

Unbeknown to me, racism was a burning issue for the police. The percentage of Maori offenders dealt with by the constabulary is wildly disproportionate to their percentage of the population and the police were copping (no pun intended) some flack for picking on Maori. This wasn't actually the case, but it had become a political hot potato so the powers-that-be were anxious to be seen doing the right thing. Hence the marae visit.

I had mixed feelings about the trip. I'd rather have spent the weekend in Palmerston North with Carey but we weren't given an option and the Maraes I'd been on before had been fun. Who knows - I might even learn something.

Unfortunately, my marae visit was a disaster of epic proportions, even on the Gonzo scale.

First day, not a problem. Got there, met the locals, rubbed a few noses, had a couple of speeches, enjoyed a sing-song and some great kai (food. Cooked in a hangi and much better than roast beef and spuds – though I did have to eat some smoked veges), immediately liked everyone, slept in the meeting house and was

167

overwhelmed by our hosts' hospitality. Brilliant.

The next day we went to Napier, visited some local schools and went to another marae in the district. It was a cool day, which was capped off with some interesting insights into the gang culture, including a discussion on why so many Maori youths ended up affiliated to the gangs. It was a refreshing perspective with talks from current and former gang members who spoke candidly of their motives for joining up. Some of us had joined the Police for similar reasons – a sense of belonging, excitement, fashion (okay, so that's pushing it a bit). It's not for nothing that the police are known as New Zealand's biggest gang.

I came away from the lectures with a new understanding about the problems Maori youth were facing. So far so good.

Then along came Saturday night. We were given a choice of things to do, which was where our instructors made their first mistake. We got into a lot less trouble when we were just told what to do.

We could volunteer to be waiters for a police function at the Civic Chambers (the boring option). We could go out with the local police for the night on a kind of station duty deal (the sensible option). Or we could go to town by ourselves (the 'potential for trouble' option). Guess which one I picked.

Nearly half the cadets opted to see what nightlife Napier had to offer and after about an hour we had all come to the same conclusion, none. We'd have to make our own fun. This meant immediately finding alcohol. Pubs were out of bounds, as the chance of a station duty cadet finding us was high and of course, we were all under age. That only left liquor stores, so a band of four of us set off to find one. It wasn't difficult - there was a store on almost every corner. Evidently we weren't the only ones to find Napier's night life a little dull.

Fozzie, Phil and Pigpen and I perused the fine range of wines, beers and spirits on display.

One of the other things I was regularly teased about at Trentham was money. I have inherited the genes of my late grandfather, Sydney Lionel Wood, and he was well known for being careful with money. He wasn't mean - quite the opposite - but he loved to find a bargain and if that meant scraping around in the sale bin then so be it. A watered down version of his blood flows in my veins and I only spend money when it is absolutely necessary.

On the night in question I found the bargain of a lifetime. Three bottles of wine were in the sale bin priced at a mere 99 cents each. I snapped up this incredible offer and told the lads our alcohol requirements were filled. They looked dubious and bought some beer in case the wine turned out to be undrinkable (a safe bet given the price).

I would be the first to admit I'm not a connoisseur and frankly, I don't know my sauvignon blanc from my beaujolais, but we weren't trying to sample the great wines of the world. We were out to get pissed and I thought these would do the job nicely. We wandered down to the waterfront along the Marine Parade and found a nice bench by the sea where we could sit and consume our goodies.

This was of course, against the law - drinking in a public place - but we seemed to have conveniently forgotten everything we'd learned about the Sale of Liquor Act. Besides, we were almost police officers now and could control our drinking. I personally controlled half a dozen beer and a bottle and a half of wine, which, as predicted, turned out to be undrinkable. Or would have been if not for the other genetic trait passed to me by Sydney Lionel. Trait 2: Once you've bought something, you have to get your money's worth no matter how crappy it turns out to be.

Once the beer was gone the other three lads tried manfully to consume the rest of the wine but the stuff was so vile they ended up tipping half of it out on to the sand. I would have been horrified had I been able to comprehend what was happening. But I couldn't. I was completely wasted and very, very sick.

Obviously I had learned nothing from the unfortunate Geoff Redfern incident and had fallen prey to the demon alcohol yet again. I'm not a big drinker so when I do partake I get drunk very quickly and then what few brains I have, go right out the window. I never get violent or destructive; instead I turn into a large helpless mass. I also have a weak stomach and a year's worth of poor diet and stress was starting to take its toll. After half an hour of heavy drinking I started to vomit. I'm not sure whether it was the quantity of alcohol or the poor quality of the wine (or both) but I was as sick as a dog.

Once I'd been vomiting continuously for an hour the other guys started to worry. By this stage I was so weak I could hardly stand. My friends decided it was time to get me back to the bus that

170

would take us back to the marae. They carried me to the bus, leant me against the side of it and left me throwing up in the gutter as the other cadets were rounded up.

I had never been so sick in my entire life. I couldn't move without feeling nauseous and was in a lot of pain from stomach cramps. The colour had washed out of my cheeks and I am told I looked like the living dead.

The other cadets didn't know what to do with me. A crowd had formed around my pathetically heaving body and discussions were being held about what action should be taken. No one wanted to tell the instructors we'd been drinking but it was obvious I needed help. They decided to get me back to the Marae as surreptitiously as possible and sneak me into bed. I was lifted into the bus and hidden in the back corner with a paper bag to throw up in and a few coats tossed on me to keep me warm. A roster was drawn up and cadets took turns checking up on me during the 20- minute trip back.

Back at the marae I was helped off the bus and propped against a nearby wall while a plan to move me into the meeting house was formulated. I started vomiting again and fell against the wall, doubled up in pain. Then I heard a sound I'd hoped not to hear. It was the voice of the chief inspector.

'What's the matter with that cadet?' he said with obvious displeasure.

He had just returned from the mayoral function at the Civic Chambers and was making his way to bed when he came across us. The chief inspector was addressing Phil, who had the presence of mind to lie brilliantly.

'That's Cadet Wood, sir. He's very sick, we think he's got food poisoning.'

Well done Phil! There was a possibility the story could be true, but the chief inspector didn't believe it for a minute and came over to have a look at me.

As he approached I turned around and did my best to stay upright. I wasn't drunk anymore - I'd vomited all the alcohol out of my system hours ago. I was just very, very ill.

As the chief inspector got closer I was struck by another huge wave of nausea and before I could say or do anything else I threw up once more, all over the chief inspector's shoes. I was too sick to realise the enormity of what I'd done but the other cadets drew in a collective gasp and waited for the world to end.

At exactly the right moment I fell onto the ground moaning, shaking and semi-conscious. This saved me from immediate expulsion. The chief inspector took one look at me and could tell I wasn't just drunk or faking it. He called an ambulance and detailed a couple of cadets to find a blanket to keep me warm until it arrived. The chief inspector turned to Phil.

'Food poisoning, you say.'

He stared long and hard at Phil before continuing. Phil held his gaze.

'Well, we'll leave it at that shall we?'

Just before leaving, the chief inspector asked Phil if he'd mind coming to the officer's hut the next morning. Phil nervously asked why. The chief inspector gave a small smile and replied. 'To clean my shoes, of course.'

I was taken straight to hospital and given an injection to stop the nausea, then I was put on a drip to stop me dehydrating. There were traces of blood in my vomit so I was placed in intensive care and watched closely until I stopped being sick. The injection worked quickly and the nausea eased off. Once my stomach settled down I was taken out of the emergency room and placed in a ward for the rest of the night, or more accurately morning. It was about 3am before I finally fell asleep.

The next day I was collected by the police and taken back to the marae. There was a day and a half left of our visit and it was felt I should join the rest of the cadets - besides the hospital wanted the bed back. I was incredibly weak from all the vomiting and couldn't hold down anything other than water. The hospital recommended I be confined to bed for the next few days so a mattress was set up in one end of the Marae's main meeting house and I was left to lie there.

I immediately fell asleep and embarrassed myself and the police as a whole by snoring loudly through the two remaining days of lectures. Apparently my timing was immaculate. Every time a Maori leader or a police representative made a deep and moving point the words were punctuated by a pig like snort or a rasping grunt from the bunk in the corner. It was undoubtedly the most culturally insensitive two days of my entire life and I don't remember a moment of it.

I was still unwell on the bus back to Trentham but as I started to recover I knew this wasn't going to be the end of the matter.

By rights I should have been thrown out of training, but Phil's quick thinking and the fact the police had no proof of my drinking saved my bacon. The hospital said I had been poisoned but were unsure as to whether it was by something I'd eaten or something I'd drunk. The instructors knew I'd been on the booze but despite my occasional lapses of judgement I was still considered to be a good cadet. I was doing well in my exams, my fitness was above the required level and I was conscientious and honest. Stupid, but honest.

A serious discussion was held by senior staff about my future and it was decided I'd be given the benefit of the doubt. I think Senior Hanley put in a good word for me and I was grateful. I really did want to be a policeman and it would have been a tragedy to have been thrown out so close to the end of the course.

As a punishment for causing the police embarrassment I was confined to barracks for the following weekend. Normally when you're confined to barracks, that's where you stay. However, on that particular weekend our wing senior sergeant and his wife had an important function and were unable to find a babysitter. Guess who? Myself and Pigpen; who was also confined to barracks for an unrelated series of offences against hygiene regulations. Not, you would have thought, the ideal pair to leave alone in your family home in charge of your loved ones. Obviously the senior sergeant was desperate. And surely we wouldn't be stupid enough to cock this up, given we were both under disciplinary clouds as it was?

I'm happy to report that no, we weren't stupid enough to get into further trouble. We sat back in his comfy lounge chairs, watched his big screen television and ate his chips without even considering the beer in the fridge or the booze in the liquor cabinet. I was right off alcohol anyway - my stomach was still dodgy from the previous weekend and any further dalliances with drink would probably have been fatal.

The kids got up a couple of times during the night so we gave them chips and fizzy drink then sent them back to bed (judging by the racket coming from the bedroom, not to sleep). This babysitting lark was a breeze. The senior sergeant had a great night out and seemed relieved that everything was in working order when he returned home. For one brief second I considered asking him for standard babysitting rates but, what with being confined to barracks and everything, it seemed a bit cheeky.

GOING BUSH

The next day there was a riot at Trentham. The Army had called our duty instructor and asked if there were any cadets available to help with an exercise they had planned for that afternoon. The scenario was as follows.

A large number of civilian youths from the surrounding districts had been gathered in the parade ground and were asked to act as protesters during a pretend commie/greenie/save the lemur type rally. The plan was that the protest would get out of hand and overrun (did he say overrun?) the thin line of police that were controlling the rally, then the army would be called in to sort things out.

The police front line was to contain about a dozen cadets, myself included, and any other cadets wanting to join the exercise could go on the protester's side. As Pigpen and I were still confined to barracks we were given no option but to be in the doomed police squad. Aqua and a few other cadets, who were around but weren't confined, thought it would be excellent fun to be protesters and have a chance to attack us.

Those of us in the police line weren't keen on facing an angry mob with no protection so we asked for full riot gear, including the new black long batons that had just been released.

We had already been given instructions on how to use the new batons or the 'black whacker,' as they were nicknamed, not for racial reasons, but because it was coloured black and you whacked people with it. The baton was two and a half times longer than the standard issue one and had a small handle on its side. It was housed on a small metal loop on your belt and in the hands of an expert it was lethal. The idea was to draw the baton out of the loop using the small side handle, flicking the baton round in a loop as you drew it and finishing with the long end tucked neatly under your elbow. Our instructor told us that when spun correctly the tip of the baton would travel at speeds in excess of 120 kilometres per hour. He personally had drawn it once on a gang member who was running at him and said when the baton slammed into the nasty man's chest' he dropped like a sack of spuds. It was later revealed the baton had shattered three of the bad guy's ribs. Choice.

Unfortunately our request for this essential equipment was denied. We were issued riot shields and could carry our standard-issue batons.

Thus armed we prepared to face the youth of the greater Wellington area (and a few turncoat cadets), in a mock riot situation. This would have been fine if some idiot from the army hadn't told the good citizens to make the riot as real as possible. They arrived armed with placards to wave and vegetables to throw, which they did with great vigour.

We huddled behind our shields and waited until the bombardment of spuds and tomatoes finished, then inched forward in a vain attempt to make them disperse.

Instead of retreating they rushed straight towards us, punching and kicking as they advanced. We were under strict orders not to hurt these alleged innocents but they clearly hadn't received the same instructions because after 10 minutes of play riot they became over-excited and began attacking us in earnest.

Once the vegetables were used up they started throwing rocks and their placards quickly turned into weapons. Several cadets were struck down, hit by stones and hunks of wood. I remember thinking 'fuck this for a game of tiddly winks' as a large rock ricocheted off the side of my shield and an ugly youth tried to push me over, ripping my uniform in the process.

Any thoughts of not harming the locals had disappeared when the first cadet went down and we hit anyone who came near us with our batons or shields. I was right in the thick of it and was being attacked on all sides by out-of-control youths. The cadets on the protester's side suddenly realised what was happening and did their best to help us. I remember seeing Aqua ripping a large stick off one of the mob as the kid tried to smash it over our unprotected heads.

The army officers finally figured out that perhaps it might be a good time for their boys to come to our aid. Amidst cries of 'about bloody time' the soldiers trooped in and charged the now rioting 'protesters'. When the mob realised the army had arrived and meant business they split up and took off, running to hide behind the barracks and dropping what was left of their placards amongst the rubble on the parade ground.

From the state of our ripped and bloody uniforms the army officers could see things had got out of control and they rushed around pretending everything had gone as planned. Fortunately no one had been seriously hurt, though most of the cadets sported cuts and bruises. I'm pleased to report some of the rioters had similar injuries, and now they had calmed down they were starting to whinge about it.

In an attempt to diffuse the situation the instructors got both sides together on the parade ground for a debriefing and some lemonade and biscuits. We stood there quietly drinking, eating, rubbing our bruises and glaring at one another. Before the volunteer youths left we were asked to shake hands with them. We did so reluctantly, only because we knew the importance of retaining good relations between the police and the public, who, I'd like to add, were trying to smash our brains out with rocks about 10 minutes earlier.

If nothing else, it was a good lesson in how quickly a supposedly peaceful demonstration can turn ugly – a lesson everyone in New Zealand would learn on a much larger scale in the coming years.

The emphasis went off the classroom in the third term as we got into practical exams with real people instead of our instructors. The police also dialled up the self-defence and endurance parts of our training. It appeared we hadn't proved our death-or-glory attitudes enough in the cart race, the raft race, the harbour swim, the marathon, a year of highly competitive sport, the rifle range, driving school or the hundreds of other activities designed to push us to our limits. Nope, what we needed now was to run through 10 kilometres of tough cross-country course with a telephone pole on our shoulders.

This wondrous event was called the poleathon. Naturally we would be racing the other sections for the honour of crossing the finish line first, just to add a competitive edge to the already treacherous nature of the race.

I don't know if you've ever lifted a telephone pole (I suspect not) but I can tell you they are bloody heavy. It would take eight to ten cadets at a time just to carry the beastly thing. Our approach was once the initial carriers got tired a fresh group would slip in and take the weight, giving the others a break.

During a practice run we discovered something very nasty about running over bumpy ground, carrying telephone poles on your shoulder - it hurts. The motion of running was bad enough because the pole bounced up and down on our shoulders, painfully bruising the bones. And because we were different heights the taller cadets got more weight on their shoulders, while the shorter ones got bashed around the ears by the movement of the pole.

Our instructors were as sympathetic as you'd expect (i.e. not at all). They told us to stick padding on our shoulders and not to be such big babies. We took the padding suggestion literally and on race day our whole section turned up looking like a squad of Quasimodo's. I had two bath towels and a pillow taped to my shoulder and my lump was nowhere near the largest. The padding had a down side - while it took a lot of pressure off your shoulder it meant that the pole bashed against the side of your head.

The course made things even more awkward - we were expected to run down muddy hills and up steep banks. This put added weight pressure on the cadets' unfortunate enough to be at the front or the rear. Half way through the run there was a particularly nasty bend on the side of a scrub-covered cliff. I was near the back of the pole and didn't realise how sharp the bend was. The runners at the front didn't realise either because they turned the corner quite sharply, forgetting their action would swing the back of the pole wide, forcing those at the rear to fall off the cliff. Four of us were pushed over the edge and we fell about five metres through mud and scrub. Every action has an equal and opposite reaction and this put too much weight on the guys carrying the front of the pole. They over balanced and fell to the ground as well.

When this happened the next 10 cadets simply swooped in, picked up the pole and carried on with the race. There was section honour at stake. One of the reserve runners did poke his head over the cliff and ask if we were alright. Upon receiving a couple of moans in the affirmative he said 'good' and buggered off as well. By the time we had picked ourselves up, dusted ourselves down and climbed to the top of the cliff, our section and our pole were half a kilometre away. We had to sprint to catch up - just in time to be handed the pole again. The entire section was shattered and bruised by the time we crossed the finish line. Some cadets had lost their towels in the run and had badly smashed their shoulders. It took over a week for us to recover from the poleathon. Physically, that is; the mental scars remain. I now have an irrational loathing of everyone who works for Telecom.

In an unrelated incident some Australian cadets came over for a visit. We beat them in the drinking competition, thanks to one cadet who has a bucket where his throat should be. That's all I'd like to say about that.

Speaking of mental scars (which I was before the Australians so rudely interrupted), shortly after our transtasman cousins left we began our bushcraft course. I recall very little of the lectures but have very strong memories of the exercise itself.

Before we plunge headfirst into my sorry tales of Trentham trekking tragedies, you should be aware of my ignominious history in the bush. I must admit, my previous attempts to commune with Mother Nature had been less than successful.

When I was a camp leader for the YMCA, our duties included teaching kids the basics of bushcraft. This was a bit difficult as I didn't know any, and to be honest my motives for spending nights in the wilderness were different from the camp director's. Where he saw it as an opportunity to teach kids some appreciation of New Zealand's native flora and fauna, I saw it as a chance to bed the female camp leaders.

My theory was that the bush was a scary place and the girls would require some masculine protection. Which just goes to show how truly stupid I was.

I had overlooked my complete and utter terror of insects. I have arachnophobia and even the tiniest spiders freak me out. I trace my terror of spiders back to primary school when the only girl in the class I actually liked turned on me one day and chased me around the classroom with a daddy long legs. Bitch. She made me look like a sissy in front of the boys and all the girls laughed. That was the last time I shared my egg sandwiches with her.

It wasn't just spiders I was afraid of. Any creepy crawly sets my nerves on edge and I especially hate flying bugs. So, as you can imagine, the bush wasn't the ideal place for me to position myself as a haven of testosterone fuelled shelter. I was less of a Bear Grylls and more of a Winnie the Pooh.

My secret was soon out but surprisingly, it worked in my favour. Several of the girls thought it 'cute' that a hulking guy like me could be reduced to a quivering wreck by a small bug and they fussed around me, making sure my bivouac was insect free. This meant they built it while I sat on a log watching. And best of all, it also meant they came in at night for a pre-sleep bug check. I even managed to persuade two girls (both of whom I had a huge crush on) that the only way I'd be safe was if they both slept in the bivouac with me. I was astonished when they agreed and I settled down for the night with a girl in each arm.

This may sound like heaven for a young heterosexual guy whose hormones were going through the roof and frankly, it was, but my joy was short lived. After about 15 minutes of having the girls snuggle up to me, one on either side, I realised that, not only was my head resting on a rock but both of my arms had gone numb. Rather than risk moving and letting go of one or both of my sleeping companions I stayed still and suffered. I was unable to sleep from the pain, so I stayed awake gritting my teeth in exquisite agony and listening to the soft plink of tree wetas falling onto the bivouac's polythene roof. Any thoughts I may had of a carnal nature (and there were many) were extinguished by the uncomfortable position I ended up in.

As I hadn't tried it on with the girls (due to both arms being dead) I got a reputation for being a nice guy. The sort of fellow girls like to be friends with. This was a disaster because, as any guy knows, friendship the kiss of death as far as sex is concerned and I never did manage to carve any notches in the tree that held up my bivouac.

Still, I was the envy of the camp for having shared the night with two women and it was all due to my new-found friends in the insect world. Though frankly, after the primary school incident, they owed me.

So, aside from discovering that rocks make extremely poor pillows, I had learnt nothing about bushcraft from the YMCA camps.

An opportunity for redemption came at army cadet training during my first sixth-form year at school. Our platoon was going to tramp through the Egmont State Forest, then on to Weld Road Reserve for Army manoeuvres. Surely, this time I would learn some useful survival techniques. Especially as there weren't going to be any female shaped distractions at this camp, mine being an all boys' school. This guaranteed the exercise was going to be a lot less fun than the YMCA camps. My bivouac companions were Geoff and Quentin and no matter how lonely it got in the bush I doubted we'd be getting together for a snuggle. We were best mates, but the line had to be drawn somewhere.

The other fun-killer was that the exercise would be taken by my biology teacher, Mr Taylor (not his real name). Not content with giving me stink marks all year, he set about making things as hard as possible for me on this tramp. He had taken a real dislike to Quentin and me. He saw us as disruptive influences, which was ironic given the rest of our platoon was made up of the school's biggest macho dickheads and hoodlums.

Naturally, as the army was in charge, they chose the worst offenders to be our platoon leaders – a small group of large second-year sixths with the most gigantic of them all (Big Gav) easily being the biggest guy in school. The others all played rugby for the first XV and were, shall we say, academically challenged. They were solid brutes and Quentin and I made it our policy to avoid them at all costs. This was difficult as they shared a loathing for Geoff, Quentin and me. Our chances of emerging from the bush intact looked bleak.

It became apparent within the first few hours that Big Gav and crew were out to get us. They opted for mental torment rather than physical. We were immediately placed on latrine duty, which meant not only digging the damn things but, even more disgustingly, filling them in after use. This group spent the 10 days giving us every shitty job their spiteful brains could think up and Mr Taylor was quite content to let them.

This unholy alliance made our lives a misery. On our first day in the bush we were taken to a particularly boggy section of ground for a lecture from Mr Taylor on swamp fauna and flora. Half way through the talk he thought of a suitably menial task for me and I was sent me off on a pointless errand. I didn't want to antagonise him so I did my best to complete the task in double quick time. My haste was to be my downfall. As I ran back towards the group I caught my foot in a supplejack vine. The creeper sprang up and catapulted me over a small bank into the swamp.

According to eye-witnesses (Quentin and Geoff) my fall was quite extraordinary as I somehow managed to fly like a spear; embedding myself head first in the swamp. I stayed vertical for a few seconds, foul-smelling water oozing into my eyes, nostrils and ears. Then, with a wet sucking squelch, my body tipped sideways and I lay sprawled in the bog. I hadn't been hurt, but I felt pretty bloody stupid.

The most astounding part of the whole incident was Mr Taylor's reaction. He was furious, and as I raised myself soggy and embarrassed from the muck he yelled at me.

'Wood! You did that deliberately to disrupt my lesson.'

I couldn't believe what I was hearing. The surrounding pupils found his claims equally ludicrous. The only thing keeping Geoff from guffawing aloud was Quentin's hand over his mouth. Taylor ranted unreasonably for several minutes but my ears were full of mud and I missed most of it. As punishment for my plot to usurp his authority I was made to sit by myself for the rest of the lesson. This ineffectual punishment was completely unnecessary because, reeking of stagnant bog water as I did, the chances of anyone sitting next to me was minimal.

Aside from latrine digging, being pushed off the occasional rock into the river by our beloved platoon leaders, and my obvious efforts to sabotage the bushcraft exercise by taking my own life, the next few days passed relatively quietly. Our nights were spent in our tents trying to sleep on bits of tree root. In contrast, Mr Taylor spent his time sharing a few beers and a smoke with Gav and the boys, their revelry only disturbed by coming over to kick the side of our tent and tell us off for talking too loud. Finally I learnt something from Mr Taylor: the meaning of the word hypocrisy.

After another three days of tramping aimlessly around the bush and having dull bits of lichen pointed out to us by Mr Taylor we finally arrived at Weld Road. Now we were onto stage two of our bushcraft exercise, which inexplicably was set in fields by the beach, miles from the bush. The army, like God, works in mysterious ways.

Our tents were much more comfortable and only had to be set up once. We had met up with the rest of the sixth form, and were split into new platoons. It appeared we were finally out of the clutches of Big Gav and pals. Yahoo.

The teachers took a back seat as the army seized control and began to teach us military stuff. This consisted of being yelled at by wiry men with short haircuts. These men were obviously very practiced at yelling and were remarkably good at it. They did strike one problem though, and it was very funny. The drill sergeants were used to screaming at grown men and had carte blanche to use whatever language they deemed fit. Said language was, however, deemed inappropriate for the delicate ears of cherubic schoolboys and the sergeants had been asked to curb their swearing.

This was like asking a dog not to lick his balls. Drill sergeants live to be offensive - they've made an art form of it and it was hilarious watching them trying to hold back and mostly not succeeding.

'What the hell sort of a fffnnn abortion are you, Wood, I've seen more coordinated cripples. Where the fffff did you learn to ffff flippen well march, fffn nursery school? You fffff fluffed up streak of weasels piss.'

Even with modified swearing, their insults were a thing of beauty and this was one part of the course that did prepare me for Trentham. Although, and I feel like a traitor for saying it, the police instructors insults weren't quite as good as the army's. No one can wound with words like the armed forces.

It turned out the army weren't going to teach us bushcraft after all - we'd already been taught that (where had I been?). Instead they were going to teach us sneaking around. A very useful skill and one I've employed many times since.

One particular form of sneaking was called the kitten crawl and it involved getting down on all fours and shuffling forward using your elbows and knees. I enjoyed this manoeuvre and decided to use it if an appropriate opportunity ever arose. My chance came the following evening on a night exercise. The aim of the activity was to sneak into a roped-off area (the enemy base), which was being patrolled by six soldiers, all armed with powerful torches and equally potent voices.

They waited until it was pitch black then began the exercise, releasing us about 500 metres away from the target area. It was up to each pupil to find their way to the enemy base without being spotted and 'shot'. If you were caught in the torch beam you had to stand up and make the long embarrassing walk to another roped-off area nicknamed 'the morgue'. There would have been more than 80 klutzy teenagers bashing about the fields of Weld Road Reserve that night and it didn't take long for the army to send at least half that number to the morgue.

Surprisingly, I was doing okay, not because of any great stealth on my part but because I'd fluked upon a sneaky route to the roped-off area. On the left hand side of the enemy base was a steep hill and I'd clambered three quarters of the way up it and was making my way along a natural ridge. I wasn't the only one using this approach but I was the only one to go so far up the hill. I could see lots of shadowy figures sneaking along the hillside below me.

Every now and then a powerful torch beam would sweep over the hill as our opponents scoured the area for movement. When this happened everyone would hit the ground and lie still.

After one particularly close call (where I was saved from

detection by a guy just below me being nabbed), I decided the best way to proceed was by utilising the kitten crawl. I assumed a prone position and began wiggling forward on my elbows and knees. This kept me low to the ground and hard to spot. But there were drawbacks, the main one being it was pitch black and I couldn't see a bloody thing. I was crawling blind. I figured I would be aright as long as I followed the line of the ridge.

This worked extremely well and before long I was closing in on the cordoned-off area. Seconds later I kitten-crawled nose first into a hedgehog. One of the nasty brute's spikes went right up my nostril. I leapt up and yelled 'Owwww fuck ow, ow, ow.'

Six torch lights hit me simultaneously. I was put on a charge for swearing (latrine duty) and sent to the morgue.

Bloody hedgehog. I decided to get my own back by biffing the prickly little bastard down the hill. I tried to pick it up but annoying beastie had rolled up into a tight ball. After fumbling around for a few minutes I finally got hold of it (spiking myself again in the process) and threw it into the night. Seconds later I heard a cry from the dark, then another, then another. On its way to the bottom the hedgehog was bouncing into members of my class who were crawling along further down the hill. It was like one of those bouncing bombs the British used to destroy dams during the Second World War. The rolling hedgehog claimed three victims before coming to a rest in the field below and scuttling off under a bush. But was it the hedgehog that got the blame for my mates capture? No, it was me and I never heard the end of it.

That was the one and only time I ever used the kitten crawl. Once again the exercise had finished without me gaining any discernible skills.

The same could not have been said for another member of our class. His name won't be revealed here to protect the guilty. Given the nature of his leanings, I'm sure he will have gone on to work for some secret government agency and is probably single-handedly reviving the Cold War.

Anyway, the classmate concerned, let's call him Mr X, had made an interesting observation. He was interested in the latrines. Not in a sick, weirdo way but in the manner of a scientific experiment (though I realise the lines quite often blur, especially given the scientific communities fixation with cloning.)

I digress. Mr X had been observing the latrines for several days and had formed an intriguing theory. He hypothesised that the long-drop style of latrine we'd been doing our business in would by now be producing a considerable amount of methane gas. Methane is a light gas and would normally disperse but Mr X thought the poor design of the long-drop holes might have resulted in small pockets becoming captured. He maintained that five days worth of school boy crap would make a decent-sized blast if ignited. Mr X proposed that some brave soul set light to a roll of toilet paper and biff it down the dunny.

We were intrigued. It was an audacious scheme and contained many elements no school boy could resist: fire, danger, an illegal act, a possible explosion and shit. How could we say no?

As it was his idea, he volunteered to do the deed. All we had to do was watch. Even better.

The set-up of the latrines was simple. Four deep holes in the ground all spilt into a trench that fed into the main bog pit. The toilets were surrounded by a five foot high wall of canvas, to preserve our modesty. This also acted as perfect shelter for anyone sneaking in and attempting to blow up the toilets. I'm surprised the army hadn't thought of this - hadn't they heard the saying 'Cripple the crapper and you cripple the camp?' Probably not, as I just made it up.

The main bog pit was Mr X's target. He'd calculated the biggest pocket of methane would be contained there and if that pocket went up then the other four bogs should follow. We were sceptical but egged him on anyway. Even the remotest chance he may succeed was more than we could resist.

At the appointed time Mr X, armed with toilet paper and cigarette lighter, sauntered into the toilet tents. We crowded around at a safe distance from the canvas wall. We didn't have to wait for long. Mr X went straight to the pit, lit the paper and, when it was nicely ablaze, he threw it down the hole.

The resulting explosions exceeded expectations. The gas in the main pit went up with a loud whoosh and a brilliant flash. A ball of fire then shot along the feeding trench, setting off four more blasts. Fountains of filthy water, bog paper, urine and large pieces of excrement, topped off with splintered toilet seats, shot high into the air.

The blast blew Mr X and the canvas wall to the ground. He landed in a heap in front of us. He was quite a sight - soaking wet and covered in shit. Astoundingly, he was uninjured and had a triumphant grin on his face. As we watched, a fine mist of sewerage rained down over the camp and a toilet seat landed on the top of the officers' mess tent. We all agreed he was entitled to smile.

After the explosion there were many accusations, threats and decidedly un-schoolboy-friendly language from the army. They badly wanted to torture the boy who had blown up their camp but as we refused to rat on Mr X (we were scared of him now) they were forced to punish the lot of us. Camp ended early that year and the entire sixth form was given a good dressing down.

And that was it. My sixth-form bush training was over and aside from my proficiency at latrine digging I had come away from the whole experience none the wiser. So, when it came to bushcraft at Trentham all I had to fall back on were the recent, highly memorable, bush survival lectures to which I'd paid no attention. There's nothing like going into the wilderness totally unprepared.

The Police, in their infinite wisdom, decided that our bushcraft survival course should be conducted in the remotest, most inhospitable area they could find. They chose the Kaimanawa State Forest. A place in New Zealand known for its wild horses and very little else.

We were driven there in the back of army vehicles, which was cool but uncomfortable. I've always thought the armed forces should make their trucks more comfy -put a bit of padding on the seats, perhaps a recliner rocker or two. This is logical if you think about it because the soldiers would be heading into battle and they would be more effective at killing people and blowing up things if they didn't have sore butts.

Anyway, there we were, all revved up for our eight days in some of the remotest bush New Zealand has to offer. We put on our army-issue rucksacks and walked for about an hour to the spot where we would set up base camp. The plan was to spend the first few days there, learning bushcraft and other handy survival tips, then we would split up into groups depending on our fitness ratings and spend the last few days tramping through the forest.

Base camp was made up of a series of tents erected in a clearing. There was an officers tent (flash), a meeting tent (flash), a cookhouse and meals tent (flash), and the cadets' tents (crap).

I was in charge of putting all the food supplies in the cookhouse tent. Typically, I managed to get all of the non-breakable stuff in without falling over but disaster struck when I was moving our supply of fresh eggs. Always on the lookout for new way to make a dick of myself I didn't do the predictable thing and drop the eggs. Instead I tripped over a frozen leg of lamb and standing on them while trying to regain my balance. The result was the same: scrambled eggs.

This made me very unpopular and at every breakfast for the rest of the week some smart-arse would comment on how nice it would be to have eggs with the bacon, followed by a universal glare in my direction.

The next day we started our Search and Rescue exercises and were shown how to make stretchers out of tree branches, splint broken limbs and construct bridges from twigs. MacGuyver eat your heart out.

Once the demonstrations were over one cadet per section was taken into the bush where he would become injured and lost. Our job was to locate him, fix him, build him a stretcher and get him back to base camp before the other sections could do the same with their injured. It was a lot of fun, or at least it was for the people carrying the stretcher. The poor wounded guy got dropped a lot because speed was deemed more important than care. If he wasn't injured at the start of the exercise, he certainly was by the end.

After Search and Rescue came Search and Destroy (it wasn't called that but that was the premise behind it). During the exercise one section would be given a roped-off area in the middle of the bush to protect while the other two sections would try and infiltrate the area. It was similar to my sixth-form exercise but much more competitive. Only one cadet was allowed to stay inside the ropes and he was compromised as soon as a cadet from any other section got inside.

The rest of the defending section had to roam outside the ropes tagging anyone they spotted. If an attacker got tagged he had to suffer the ignominy of sitting with the instructors until the game ended. The exercise finished when the defending section's area was successfully invaded or the other sections' players were all tagged.

195

It was a great game which I enjoyed enormously, even though my natural clumsiness ensured I was tagged before getting close to the target. As one of the instructors unkindly pointed out, I moved through the bush with the stealth of a charging rhinoceros. I was better at catching people and our section held the others at bay for the longest time, winning the exercise.

It was really windy the next day which was a bugger because we were supposed to go abseiling. I had never done it and fancied a go. Given my propensity for injury it was probably a good thing it was cancelled. Instead we prepared ourselves for the three-day tramp that was to begin the following day.

We were split into groups depending on fitness levels and I was in the slowest group. Aqua and Phil drew the short straw by being in the next group up which was to be taken by the nastiest, most sadistic instructor in the college. I thought this was very funny as I knew he'd walk the legs off them and they'd spend their entire tramp marching through the bush.

My instructor, on the other hand, was the nicest guy there and I was sure we'd end up having a gentle stroll through the forest. Nope. Our instructor saw the bushcraft exercise as an opportunity to prove that he was as hard as the rest of the instructors and spent the entire three days walking the guts out of us.

In a cruel twist of fate, Phil and Aqua's group ended up having the cruisiest time of all. The evil instructor started, as I'd predicted, by making them complete a four hour trek in just two hours but then his plans went horribly wrong. He'd pushed his troop so hard that

Phil got really bad blistering on his feet - so bad that he was unable to walk any further. His instructor had a fit, claiming Phil had sabotaged the tramp and had ruined it for everyone else. Then he stomped off to radio headquarters for permission to leave Phil alone in the bush. Dickhead.

Thankfully, headquarters said he couldn't desert Phil and they instructed him to set up camp where they had stopped (an idyllic little valley). He was told to leave Phil at base to recuperate while he took the others on day tramps. He was furious, but there was nothing he could do about it so he sulked and let the cadets walk around doing whatever they wanted.

Phil became an instant hero and proudly showed his blistered feet to all the other, completely knackered troops who passed through their valley. My group came through at the end of a solid eight-hour march during the second day. I was disgusted to see Phil and Aqua relaxing by a stream. We stopped for a 10-minute break, which Aqua spent laughing and pointing out the irony of the situation, then we were off for another two hour's solid marching before collapsing into bed.

The constant tramping was bad enough, but the worst thing for me was the hunger. I'd stuffed up badly. When we were issued with our rations (standard army field packs), I'd gone through my kit with a fine tooth comb. I instantly identified the things I knew I didn't like and swapped the offending articles for foodstuffs I liked to eat.

As all the food came in sachet form, the identification process came down to the description on the packet. I knew instantly that 'lamb curry' wouldn't be for me, 'beef stew' had onions listed in the ingredients so that was out; and 'steak and vegetables' had the V word in it so that was a no-go as well. The only thing that sounded any good was 'ham and egg omelette', so I rushed around all the cadets swapping my meaty cast-offs for their ham and egg omelettes. By the time we set off all I had in my ration kit were army biscuits, dried raisins, a tube of honey and two dozen sachets of 'ham and egg omelette'.

Lunch time on the first day of the tramp was the first opportunity we had to try our dried meals. We all added boiling water to our sachets and waited eagerly for the taste sensation that was to follow. I realised the enormity of my mistake when I placed a spoonful of a congealed tasteless crap, which was supposed to be an omelette, in my mouth. A fouler, more inedible substance I have never found.

One of the other cadets in my group had held onto of his ham and egg omelettes sachets and he also tried it at lunchtime. Word of the omelette horror spread quickly and within minutes there was no way anyone would swap back with me. I was stuck with three days' worth of inedible meals and everyone in the group, including the instructor (who I was rapidly going off), thought it was hilarious.

To compound matters, the other groups had also discovered that the omelette was to be avoided like the plague so even when we ran into them my pleading for a trade was met with derisive laughter. That left me with biscuits, raisins and honey. Not a very substantial meal for the amount of tramping we were doing.

To make matters worse the biscuits were as hard as the hobs of hell and you could never tell which would break first, your teeth or the biscuit. Phil was relatively sympathetic when we ran into him. He wouldn't swap any of his rations, but he did give me his tube of honey and a few more biscuits.

Towards the end of the second day's tramping I was close to passing out from exhaustion and starvation. Fortunately our instructor shot a deer and cooked it over a fire for dinner. It was the most delicious meat I'd ever tasted. I don't know whether it was my ravenous hunger, two days' worth of eating poxy army biscuits, or the freshness of the meat and the open-fire cooking that made it so tasty, but I've never had venison since that has come close.

Tales of my traumatic culinary experiences spread through the wing upon our return and the irony of me being stuck with only omelettes to eat when I had destroyed everyone else's eggs was not lost on most people.

THE WORST CAR IN THE WORLD GETS WORSE

When we got back to Trentham we took drugs. It was part of our final classroom unit on dangerous and illegal substances. We had a sniff and a quick puff of cannabis so we would know what it smelt and tasted like.

We also got to rub cocaine on our teeth though I've never been able to figure out why. I couldn't taste anything and it just made my teeth feel gritty. Still, it was what they wanted so why argue?

As part of the unit we had a lecture from an undercover drugs cop. He was very interesting but some of the things he told us made me feel quite depressed. So it's only fair that I pass it on to you.

He told us about junkies who had destroyed the veins in their arms so badly they had to shoot up in other parts of the body, including between their fingers and toes and even into their eye lids. He told us some undercover cops get so involved in the drug scene that they become hooked on heavy drugs and have to go through hell to clean up. His lecture was a mixture of horror stories, gore and hopelessness. And though it was fascinating it put me right off drugs.

There was however, a fix I desperately needed. I hadn't seen

Carey for several weeks. First there had been the marae visit, then I was confined to barracks, and finally we had gone bush. I was definitely in need of a trip to Palmerston North. The following weekend was not a leave weekend but the Saturday night inspection of the cadet barracks had stopped and the rules had loosened up enough for me to feel that going AWOL was worth the risk.

As I've mentioned, it was pretty hard to get kicked out and I wasn't even on a final warning. I figured if they caught me I'd get an ear-bashing and would probably be confined to barracks for the next few weekends but that would be all.

I drove up to Palmerston North on the Saturday morning but had a few problems with Floyd's brakes during the trip. When I arrived at Quentin's place he told me he thought the brakes needed bleeding and volunteered to help. I was surprised Quentin had agreed to assist me. He said he felt sorry for me and that a mate's a mate, even if he does have the crappiest car in the world.

Quentin isn't known for his mechanical abilities but his diagnosis made sense. On the way down I'd had to pump the brakes to make them go and this was an indicator of air in the brake lines. Q said while I was visiting Carey he'd have a chat with a mate of his who knew about these sorts of things and we'd fix the problem upon my return.

Carey and I spent the morning becoming re-acquainted then spent the afternoon becoming re-acquainted again.

I got back to Quentin's flat late in the afternoon to find him keen to have a go at Floyd's brakes. He had his tool kit out and had bought a large plastic syringe. I was reluctant to ask him what the syringe was for but in the end couldn't help myself. Apparently we we're going to pump up the brakes then release the air and fluid via the appropriate nipples. The syringe would be used to squirt more fluid into the brake cylinder that was housed under the bonnet.

I was impressed. Quentin had obviously done his homework and before long we had all the brakes properly bled. All that was left to do was fill the brake fluid cylinder with new liquid, using the syringe. There wasn't much room under Floyd's bonnet and it was a struggle getting to the appropriate cylinder, which was at the back.

After one successful squirt Quentin refilled the hypodermic and passed it to me but as he was backing out from underneath the crowded bonnet he bumped my elbow, knocking the syringe out of my hand.

The syringe dropped neatly into the brake cylinder and sank to the bottom. We tried for about an hour to get the damn thing out but gave up in the end, reasoning it wasn't blocking the fluid intake hole so it couldn't do any harm. I stuck the cylinder cap back on and forgot about it.

On the way back to Trentham the following night, I noticed that Floyd was running rough - the brakes were functioning okay but I figured the syringe in the cylinder must be causing other problems. The car would run well for a few minutes then it would give a jerk and lose power before kicking into action again. Anyone with an ounce of mechanical knowledge would have worked out this couldn't be down to the rogue syringe, but not me. I simply resigned myself to another bumpy trip and decided to get Floyd fixed when I got back.

I didn't get back.

An hour out of Trentham Floyd's lights suddenly cut out and all the electrics failed, shutting the engine down. 'This is bad,' I thought as the car glided to the side of the road. I sat in the silent car wondering how a syringe could cause such carnage then it dawned on me that perhaps it wasn't the syringe after all. I got out of my vehicle and was just about to look under the bonnet when, for some reason, I decided the trouble may be in the boot, where the battery is located.

This decision may have saved my life. I went to the back of the car and opened the boot. The handle was hot when I touched it, which was surprising. As the trunk popped open I realised why. My car was on fire. Holy Shit! And it wasn't just a small blaze - there was a raging inferno inside my boot.

As I watched, a plastic can full of oil exploded in a ball of flame, singeing my eyebrows. I recoiled in shock wondering what the hell to do. Then I noticed that the half-full can of petrol I kept in the boot (a bomb waiting to go off) was sitting in the middle of the flames. The can expanded outwards with a sickening click, the way things do right before they explode.

I knew if the can went up it would be all over. The car's petrol tank was located in the back and I could hear a hissing noise coming from under the petrol cap. If I didn't put the fire out in a hurry I'd see a car explode in extreme close up.

The other option was to run like hell and let it blow. This would have been the sensible thing to do, but Floyd and I had been through a lot together - I couldn't just desert him.

As I reached into the flames and grabbed the patrol can it clicked again and expanded under my hands. It was seconds away from detonation. I hauled it out of the boot as quickly as I could and hurled it down the road. It sailed through the air, landed on the concrete and exploded with a loud boooff, shooting a small ball of flame into the air. Had I not been so worried about the bonfire still blazing in my boot I would have been hugely impressed.

I rushed back to the car, grabbed a blanket from the back seat and set about beating out the flames. I had quite a battle on my hands as the blanket kept catching fire but after several minutes of furious beating I had everything under control.

When I was sure the fire was out I collapsed by the side of the road. I needed to catch my breath and survey the damage. The blanket was smouldering beside me, my jersey was black and singed and I'd burnt my fingers when pulling the petrol can out of the fire, but aside from that I was okay.

Floyd wasn't quite so lucky. I waited for the metal in the boot to cool down then examined the damage. The trunk was full of melted and burnt things and as I laid the unfortunate items on the road beside the car I worked out what had happened. The syringe had nothing to do with it. Instead, the blaze was due to plain bad luck and the fact that I'm messy and disorganised. A metal screwdriver I had flung into the boot sometime in the past had fallen across the two exposed points of the car battery, causing a spark. The spark set fire to an oily rag that I had carelessly left lying around in there. The cloth in turn ignited various other bits of rubbish that littered the boot.

Once the fire began it burnt through the electrical wires that fed off the battery, causing the lights and everything else to cut off. This was what saved me - otherwise I would have been driving merrily along until the petrol can and then the petrol tank exploded. I must have been minutes away from that happening. On examining the debris from the boot I noticed that the fire had been so intense that the head of the screwdriver had burnt a hole right through a metal hub cap.

On surveying the melted and twisted mass of wires in Floyd's boot, I correctly judged my car would be going no further that night. I had no option but to leave it on the side of the road. This left me with a dilemma. It was eight o'clock in the evening, I was stranded miles from Trentham and I was AWOL.

As I sat beside Floyd trying to decide what to do, a police car pulled up. Oh great, I thought. Just what I need. A passing motorist had seen me battling the flames and had reported the incident to the local cops.

They were bloody good once I explained who I was. A lift back to Trentham was organised for me through a relay of police cars, and a tow truck was arranged to retrieve poor crippled Floyd. They even radioed ahead to let the duty Sergeant know what had happened, though my story of just being out for a Sunday drive caused a few raised eyebrows. I got away with it as the duty instructor was so overcome with the apparent hilarity of the incident (I was the only one not laughing) that he was prepared to buy my weak cover story.

I flopped down onto a chair in Mark's room. 'That was definitely the worst trip I've ever had.'

After my near-death experience I reluctantly decided Floyd had to go. The next weekend I made the long trek back to New Plymouth to seek Dad's help. With my car firing on two cylinders, I limped home then handed Dad the keys and said 'Do what you have to do.' Dad understood. He took Floyd out to the back of the farm and shot him, humanely, in the head gasket. I cried for a week.

Okay. What actually happened was Dad sold him to some poor deranged individual for $400, and I celebrated for a week. Then Dad got his mate (the same mate who sold me Floyd) to find me another car. He came back with a dark red Mark Two Ford Cortina which made suspicious noises.

Assured it was fine and lacking the mechanical knowledge to argue the point, I bought the car and called it Clyde after the orangutan in Clint Eastwood's movies (I should have called it Lassie because it was a dog and it broke down twice on the way back to Trentham). Arriving late on Sunday I trudged into Mark's room and told him I had a new car, it was called Clyde and was directly related to Floyd. There was no need to say anything else.

One good thing came out of Clyde's arrival at Trentham - it

gave us another opportunity to tease Wayne.

Wayne had a very sensible car, an Avenger, which was his pride and joy. He refused to name it, that would have been silly, and because it was such a boring vehicle we had been unable to come up with an appropriate moniker. Wayne's car was parked between my car and Aqua's car which is how we solved the naming dilemma. Aqua's car was called Bonnie, so when I arrived with Clyde, the name for Wayne's car became obvious - we called it 'And'. 'And the Avenger'. Wayne suddenly came up with a raft of new names for his car but to no avail. He was destined to spend the rest of his days at Trentham driving around in a car named after a joining word.

Trentham carried on regardless of our car dramas and General Poananga, the patron of our wing, popped in for a visit. The year was nearly finished and it was the only time we ever saw him. He seemed a nice enough chap and was obviously chuffed at having a police cadet wing named after him. I was confused as to why an army officer was our patron but what the hell; the army had saved me (eventually) from being battered to death during our mock riot so it was cool by me.

As our class work eased up, the emphasis was placed on our fitness. Our instructors were determined to have us finish the course in top shape. I was the fittest I'd ever been, having just finished a gruelling cross-country run (which stuffed poor old Phil's knees for a week) and then competing in a relay race through a nearby valley.

There had been no way to get out of it, or cheat, so I gritted my teeth and ran my part as required. I'm pleased I did because I ran faster than I had ever run before and felt great while doing it. There's nothing like being 18 and in peak physical condition. It's much better than being 51, and knackered with a dodgy calf, a bung shoulder and a wobbly ankle.

The end was in sight. There were no more trips lined up so it would be difficult for me to sabotage my career. In fact it would have been damn near impossible to fail now. Or so we thought.

On the fourth of November, just one month out from graduation, the seventh and final cadet to be thrown out of Trentham was expelled for the relatively minor offence of being caught drinking under-age in a bar in Upper Hutt. He had been warned for this offence several times during the year, and I assume it was his disregard for these cautions that saw him removed from the police. He was a very popular cadet and it was a big blow to the morale of his section to see him go. To have survived 11 months of Trentham and be dismissed just before the end must have been heartbreaking. We thought his punishment was particularly unfair as several other cadets were drinking with him and they only received warnings. The other cadets had very good academic and behavioural records and I think that is what saved them. Still, it was a cruel blow and one from which we never forgave the top brass. His expulsion did have one positive effect. It reinforced our vulnerability and everyone knuckled down, determined not to go the same way.

The last month passed quickly as we finished our academic syllabus, completed our final RFL, and began swotting for our final exams. It became obvious no further cadets were expected to fail when we were asked to apply for our postings for the following year - our first year as real policemen. We had to name three preferences for postings but were told every effort would be made to give us our first choice.

My elected location was Palmerston North (surprise!), my second was New Plymouth and my third was Wellington. In a bizarre move, we were given the results of our placements before we had completed our exams but were told these were provisional postings and dependent on our successful completion of the course.

My posting was Palmerston North. I was rapt. I rang Carey, she was pleased. I rang Mum and Dad, they were delirious with joy. The thought of their son with police powers in the same town as them would have been too much to bear.

The exams were stressful but everyone had swotted so hard it was inconceivable we'd fail. No-one did.

On the official front all that was left to do was to prepare for graduation. On a personal level there were a few things that needed closure. The first was something we'd been threatening to do all year. Aqua, Phil, Pigpen and I were going to nugget Wayne's eyebrows.

Tidy, blond, 'never a hair out of place,' Wayne was about to get what he deserved - black eyebrows. Wayne had laughed at our promise to do this dreadful deed and he refused to believe we'd go ahead with it. The laughter stopped when we charged into his room, pinned him to the bed and brought out the boot polish. He struggled but we held on and before long Wayne had a whole new look.

Photos were taken as evidence, cadets were paraded in for inspection, then finally, Wayne was released to rush to the bathroom and scrub himself back to pristine condition.

Next came graduation. All our friends and rellies would be there for our big day and the police were going to make sure they put on one hell of a display for them. More accurately, they were going to make sure we did.

Some genius, who had obviously never seen us on the parade ground, decided C Section was going to put on a precision marching display. The word 'precision' had never been applied to our marching before and I wondered how they were going to achieve this miracle. By having us practise four hours a day until we got it right, that's how. The display required us to complete a complex series of manoeuvres without any audible instruction. This meant learning the moves off by heart and pacing them out as we went. Phil and I had a lot of trouble with this and we were given individual tuition after hours. By graduation we could perform the manoeuvres in our sleep.

I was also in the trampolining display as I was quite good at gymnastics. I had little style or grace but technically I was very good, able to perform somersaults and half-pikes with the best of them. Our section was also called upon to give a horse-vaulting display. I was good at vaulting too, able to complete some flashy moves, but for the graduation demonstration we only had to do was a straightforward vault, simply on and off the horse, all the cadets in one impressive stream.

On the day there would also be self-defence displays and a demonstration of the effectiveness of the new black batons. This was to be a choreographed incident in which an offender attacks a police cadet with a baseball bat. The cadet would ward off the blows with his baton then subdue the offender by sweeping his legs from underneath him. All very impressive except on the second day of training the cadet defending himself swung the baton incorrectly and exposed his forearm to the swinging bat. The bat smashed into his arm, shattering the bone and the cadet ended up in hospital, destined to spend the rest of his training, graduation and the holiday season in a plaster cast.

Undeterred, the gym instructor simply replaced the injured cadet with another 'volunteer'. The instructor didn't care - there were still 70 of us left if need be. Fortunately the next guy avoided serious injury and the baseball bat versus long baton demonstration was one of the highlights of the day.

Our marching display went without a hitch, to much 'oohing' and 'aahing' from the crowd - even Mum waving at me didn't put me off my step.

The horse vault was a different kettle of fish. I wasn't worried about it at all. I'd done the vault hundreds of times and was capable of much harder manoeuvres, yet somehow I blew my approach and hit the springboard too hard. My legs were up too high and I was in danger of falling in a crumpled heap on the ground, right in front of my family, friends and the love of my life. There was a gasp from the crowd as it appeared I was going to terminate myself and a sigh of relief as I somehow managed to twist my body back into line, in time to hit the mat rolling in what must have looked like a planned move. It wasn't and it hurt like hell.

'Nice recovery.' the gym instructor whispered to me as I went past. Yeah, nice recovery, shame about my back.

The rest of the day went smoothly and just after lunch the graduating class of the 24th General Poananga Police Cadet Wing marched proudly through Upper Hutt to the town hall to be sworn in as police officers.

I'd graduated. Despite everything I'd done to prove I was incapable of such responsibility, the police decided otherwise.

The graduation ceremony was full of pomp and speech-making. Next was the swearing-in - we all soberly promised to do the right thing and be good little policemen. Then we threw our hats in the air, our Mums cheered and that was it. We were fully empowered officers of the law.

It was an anti-climax after everything we'd been through. We didn't know what to do with ourselves. We'd survived a year at Trentham because of the support of our mates. Now we were about to be torn apart and sent all over the country to fend for ourselves. Our umbilical cords had been severed for a second time.

I felt completely unprepared for what was to come. And I was.

It wasn't anyone's fault - my instructors had done an excellent job and I knew the law backwards. I was the fittest I'd ever been and had the skills I needed to be a policeman. The problem was I hadn't finished being a kid yet. I was blissfully unaware of what was to come and the excitement of completing Trentham and becoming a police officer would take a long time to fade.

The day after graduation our instructors waved us off, confident they were sending forth a troop of highly trained professionals, all ready and willing to carry the banner proudly for the New Zealand Police.

Forgive them, for they knew not what they did.

POLICE CONSTABLE WOOD 7389

I had been 19 for a month and seven days when I became a sworn-in member of the New Zealand Police. I wasn't allowed to see R20 movies, I couldn't drink in a pub by myself and I was still two years away from receiving the key to adulthood on my 21st birthday. I could, however, take away your car keys, your drugs, your money, your property, your right to work, your standing in the community and your freedom.

I failed to see any irony in the situation and couldn't wait to get started. I had to. The police had given me three weeks holiday which I was obliged to take. Not a bad idea given the rigours of Trentham and the demands from my family and girlfriend for some quality time. I too wanted quality time, but not with them. Instead hooked up with a mate of mine from New Plymouth and went to Christchurch.

We picked Christchurch because that was where Phil lived and he said we could stay at his parents' place for free. This turned out to an unpopular move with almost everybody (especially Phil's parents). Mum and Dad were peeved they couldn't show me off for longer than a few days (though I did promise to be home for Christmas), and Carey was livid. I tried to explain that I needed some space for a few weeks and that we'd have plenty of time together once I got to Palmerston North, but she was still mad I'd chosen to spend my break away from her.

The situation wasn't helped by the friend I'd elected to spend time with. His name was Nigel and he was a great guy, though possibly the maddest person I've ever known. He was one of those blokes whose exploits become legendary.

Nigel had come to my graduation and surprised everyone by spending the evening waltzing beautifully with my grandmother, then returning to the motel and sleeping in the wardrobe, for no reason other than he thought it might be a cool thing to do.

He and Carey disliked each other instantly. Probably because the first time he met her was at a barbeque at her parent's place where he turned up uninvited. Actually, to be fair, I had invited him but, neglected to mention this to Carey, so technically he was a gate-crasher. This worried Nigel not a jot and he had a great time scoffing most of the food and leaping off the roof of Carey's parent's house into their swimming pool. This particular feat of craziness had never been attempted before but proved a big hit on the night. With me anyway. I was hugely impressed and was surprised to discover later that I had been the only one.

The thing that worried Carey the most about Nigel was his madness was infectious and, much to Carey's family's disgust, it didn't take long for me to join him in the roof leap. And Nigel had been on his best behaviour that night, which gives you some idea how lethal he could be when he wasn't. Such as our jaunt to the South Island (the details of which remain sealed under the official secrets act). It had been exactly the sort of break I needed. One last fling of full-on craziness before the full weight of my new responsibilities bore down on me.

I was due to start my new job in Palmerston North on the 31 December, a start date dictated by the police needing extra cops on the beat during New Years Eve.

I was excited and fearful about the start of my career. But starting my new job wasn't the only thing I had to worry about - there was the small matter of finding somewhere to live. As luck would have it one of Quentin's teachers' college friends had a boyfriend who was also looking for a flat. His name was Warren but everyone called him Sheep because of his blond shaggy hair and full white beard. I'd met him before at teachers' college functions and we'd always got on really well. He was interested in flatting with me (the fool) and we decided to give it a go.

The next day we sat down over a few beers and made a list of the things both of us could bring into a flatting situation. He had a really loud stereo, some pies and a beanbag. I had cassettes, I liked pies and I too owned a bean bag. A match made in heaven. With the entertainment and furniture sorted out, all we had to do was find an appropriate rental property. After a 2 second search we found a four-bedroom house in a dodgy area just out of town. It had a pub nearby and not a lot else to recommend it but we couldn't be stuffed looking any further so we rented it.

The baker and the policeman - both first-time flatmates, both under 20, both earning good money, both with girlfriends living elsewhere in the city, both keen on beer and fatty food. The stage was set. Heaps of fun but, oh, the damage done. Especially to my long-term health. But I was 19 at the time and my idea of long term was next week.

So, I was set up in Palmerston North with a friend to flat with, the love of my life not far away, my police career about to start and, best of all, a brand new car. Clyde was no more. It had broken down one time too many and after putting a new engine in it (from Dad's mate who sold me Floyd and Clyde), I sold it to a pal of mine from New Plymouth.

Now I had to buy another new car. This time I was prepared. I had a plan. First I made sure Dad wasn't involved. Second, I picked a car that wasn't red or pink or any pigment thereof, and finally I gave my new car a much tougher-sounding name. I became the proud owner of a 1.6 litre Mark Three Ford Cortina, coloured yellow with the very cool moniker of Cortez the Killer, after a Neil Young song.

This was definitely a 'kick ass' name for a 'kick ass' car, although Carey took some of the testosterone of out my sails by claiming it looked lovely and would be comfortable on trips. Still, I was master of my own domain and ready to show the world - or Palmerston North to start with - what Glenn Wood could do.

The first thing I did was hide.

As mentioned earlier, I was due to start on New Year's Eve so my first shift was a night shift. I was incredibly nervous. I must have ironed my shirt 20 times and I'd cleaned my shoes so often I'd run out of spit.

My shift was due to start at 9pm but I arrived at the station half an hour earlier to make a good impression. There was no-one around to make a good impression on as my section didn't arrive until five to nine and everyone else was out on patrol or too busy to worry about me. I got a few scattered hello's and then went and sat in the lunch room to practice setting my handcuffs on the last click.

I had already met most of the people in my section during an earlier introductory day. Keith (our go kart pilot) was there too. He was the only other cadet posted to Palmerston North and he'd been put in a different section to me. During the introduction we had been shown around the station by a senior sergeant and then introduced to our respective section members. After that we were given a rundown on how the sections worked and what everyone's jobs were. We already knew most of this but we listened eagerly anyway.

There were eight members to each section, including one sergeant and at least three senior constables (if you were lucky). Of the eight, one would be in charge of the operations centre and they would be responsible for taking incoming calls and dispatching officers to the various jobs. Two of the others would take out the I Car - incident car - which would be the first dispatched to any incidents. Another pair of officers would cruise around in a mobile beat car. Their job was to back up the I Car or attend jobs themselves if the shift became busy.

The remaining two officers were dispatched on foot, or on

'the beat' in Police lingo. The beat officer's job was general policing around the city centre, which meant making sure all the shops were securely locked and that order was kept in the streets.

The sergeant took out his own car and turned up where and when he was needed. In addition to the section on duty there was generally an E car, (enquiry car) on patrol, plus a team policing unit on Friday and Saturday nights. This unit consisted of 10-12 large and brutal officers who were dispatched into the city's worst trouble spots, or pubs as they are more commonly known.

Dog handlers appeared occasionally as well. You could never be sure when, as they were a law unto themselves and seemed to have no set working patterns. Generally they turned up when you called them and worked when they felt like it. There were also a few detectives, drug squad members and senior officers floating about, working to agendas the rest of us weren't privy too. That was the rough make-up of the station at any given time.

The other reason we were called in for our introductory day was so Keith and I could get our police drivers licence. This turned out to be as simple as we'd been promised - we both drove around the block without hitting anything or killing anyone and were duly awarded our licences. Keith and I were then split up to spend a couple of hours with our new colleagues.

I was teamed up with one of the younger members of my section, who took me for a drive around the city, or more accurately around to his place so he could pick up his lunch. He was as young and stupid as I was and drove like a hoon, yelling out the window to girls as we drove past. He was just showing off in front of the new boy and when he noticed I was more bewildered then impressed he settled down. We arrived back at the station later that day in time for everyone to rush off again with the sergeant hurriedly telling me he'd see me on New Year's eve.

So there I was, sitting by myself in the lunchroom, feeling confused and totally out of my depth. As I was to quickly discover, I wasn't the only one.

The rest of my section finally arrived and introductions were made again. My sergeant was an older guy who had been in the job for years but, as I found out later, his heart wasn't really in it anymore and he was looking for a way out. The senior cops in my section included a Policewoman who hated me on sight, a grouchy, morose guy with a drinking problem (nicknamed Crusty), and a chap in his early forties who, thank God, was a decent bloke.

The three younger officers included the not-yet-grown up hoon I'd met earlier, a very pleasant but under confident guy in his early twenties and a decent, hardworking cop who wanted to become a dog handler. Not the most inspiring bunch of workmates I'd ever seen, but beggars can't be choosers and I'd have to make the best of the situation.

Just how dodgy the situation would become was apparent when the night's roster was read out. I was on the beat by myself. I couldn't believe it - this was my first night as a policeman and they were sending me out on my own, on New Year's Eve. I was told I'd be checked on regularly but the section was stretched too thin to double up. There was no gentle introductions to police work for me. I wasn't going to be mollied or coddled. I was in boots and all.

I picked up my RT 9no mobile phones in those days), set it to the appropriate channel and slunk out of the station.

The streets were really busy and I decided on my course of action for the evening as soon as I got outside. If people didn't bother me I wouldn't bother them. My definition of 'people' being 'the general public', whom I was supposed to be serving.

I got through the first few hours without having to interact very much with anyone and was relieved when it was time to go back to the station for my dinner break.

The rest of the section were having a busy night and they rushed in and out. Several of my new workmates asked how I was going and the Sergeant said he'd join me after midnight, if things quietened down.

I snuck out of the station again at half past 11 and moped around the back streets checking buildings for break-ins. This gave me time to think and I was starting to get my confidence back. Obviously the sergeant trusted me; otherwise I wouldn't be out here by myself. Besides, I'd just finished a year at Trentham and was in top physical shape. Yeah, I could handle this. I knew the law backwards and had the power of the law behind me. As the clock struck twelve I was Cinderella going to the ball.

I puffed up my chest and strode into the square, just as a horde of drunken students poured out of a van. They were having a great night and as it turned midnight the girls in the group went looking for someone to kiss. They found me and four very attractive young ladies dived on me, knocking my hat off and covering me with New Year kisses. Normally I would have enjoyed this but was terrified my new Sergeant would come around the corner and see me buried under a pile of floozies. I could hear him now.

'Constable Wood, put those women down immediately and report to my office.'

It was my first night on the job and I was going to be fired for sexual misconduct. I didn't know what to do. The textbooks hadn't covered this sort of thing. All I could think of was Jacko's immortal words 'Women, Boy!'. I did my best to extricate myself from their embraces but they were determined young minxes and apparently I wouldn't be allowed to leave until I'd kissed them all.

I toyed with the idea of arresting them for having offensive lips but as this clearly wasn't the case I had no option but to pucker up and get it over with as soon as possible.

They quickly tired of making me blush and ran off, the last girl pausing to mess up my hair, put my hat back on and plant a final peck on my cheek before scooting off to join her mates.

I stood there with a stupid smile on my face before remembering I was supposed to be protecting the public from this sort of lewd going-on. I rushed back to the station and spent the next couple of hours in hiding until my sergeant found me and made me go out again.

At precisely 3.12am I got my first call on the radio.

'Beat from ops.'

They had to say it again before I realised they were talking to me.

'Beat from ops.'

I replied as we'd been taught.

'Beat, ten three, Cuba Street.'

Ten three meant I was patrolling freely and had no jobs on the go.

'Yeah Beat, we've had a report of a large semi-naked Maori in the square. He is carrying a large spear. Can you check this out please?"

'Roger, on my way.'

I sounded much calmer than I felt. Great, what a fine end to the evening, I was going to be punctured by some drunk, naked bloke on my first night on the beat.

I spent an hour looking (not very hard) for the guy but was unable to find him. At 4am my sergeant came to give me a hand and immediately located the offender. We were sneaking through some bushes and the Sergeant stopped suddenly.

'There he is!' he cried, pointing into the night.

'Where?' I said, straining my eyes in the darkness. I couldn't see anyone. The town square was deserted.

'There!' he said jabbing his finger forward.

Then I saw him. The giant, fierce, heavily armed man was a large bronze statue of a Maori warrior.

Oh, ha, ha, ha.

We went back to the station and everyone thought it was hilarious. Once the mirth had died down, we sat drinking coffee until the next shift arrived. It had been a quiet New Year's Eve, with hardly any trouble and few arrests. I was told I'd be placed in the I car the next night, then everyone drifted home.

That was the end of my first night in the New Zealand Police. I had survived with minimal embarrassment and no major cock-ups. But don't worry; there was plenty of time for that in the months to come.

YOU'RE UNDER ARREST

I found out in my first week that being a policeman was much harder than being a cadet. I don't know why I was surprised.

The thing I was having the most trouble getting to grips with was how little fun it was. Only three people in my section had a sense of humour and there wasn't much section spirit. Sure, everyone backed each other up when we were working but there weren't many friendships within the group. Maybe that was just what it was like in the police. If so, it was very different from Trentham, where your workmates were also your best buddies.

All these years later and even though I'm no longer in the police, I can still call up several of my Trentham mates for a chat, but there is only one person from my time in Palmerston North I keep in contact with, or have any desire to. I can only think of four people out of the whole station who I would like to see again. It's a shame really because it was a time when I could really have done with some friends at work.

My mates outside the police were a different story. Sheep and I were getting on like a house on fire (almost literally several times) and we were coping with the flat, even though several inadequacies had become glaringly obvious.

Our choice of location could have been better. I'd seen our street name on several arrest sheets and we'd definitely camped in an 'interesting' neighbourhood. It wasn't a bad street but was working class and had its fair share of characters, our next-door neighbours being one of them. This became obvious the day after we moved in. It was a Saturday morning and we were woken by a dog barking and then a sharp yelp. Sheep and I got up and made it to the back yard in time to hear our next door neighbour shriek at her kid: 'Jeffrey, take that screwdriver out of the dog's ear!'

Sheep and I looked at each other and decided to retire back into the house. Having said that, we had no trouble from our neighbours the whole time we flatted there, although having a police car parked in our front yard every now and then probably helped. Half the neighbourhood thought we were cops and the other half thought we were crims. I don't know which impressed them the most.

The other issue that surfaced early in our flatting life (aside from our lack of furniture, which worried our girlfriends a lot more than it worried us) was our combined abilities on the culinary front. Being a baker, Sheep was good with all things pastry and he could cook a mean roast. I, on the other hand, had little or no cooking ability, which I demonstrated by asking him how much fat you put in the frying pan to poach eggs.

My diet had not improved - if anything it got worse. There was a constant supply of pies and sausage rolls in the fridge courtesy of Sheep, and I was drinking more than I ever had before (or have since). Sheep, and I even went to the extreme of pouring Creme de Cacao liquor on our ice cream at night - the height of decadence for a couple of young lads in their first flat.

I have photos of our house in those days and one shows the interior of our fridge. The top shelf contained a jug of gravy, a brown lettuce, a chub of luncheon sausage, a pie, butter and a jar of jam. The next three shelves contained beer, oh, and a cask of wine for the girls. I'm sure this was typical of a lot of flats in Palmerston North but Sheep and I had the combined income to make sure it stayed this way.

Other friends on their way back to Palmerston North for the start of the year included Quentin, who was going to Massey University to muck around while pretending to study for a Batchelor of Arts degree, and Carey who was due back at Teachers College for her second year.

I was really looking forward to Carey's return as we would finally be in the same city and would be able to spend a lot more time together. I had also made friends with Quentin and Carey's mates and had a big circle of pals outside the police. Strangely enough, the police saw this as a negative and I was told off for spending too much time with students and not enough with my section. Perhaps if they'd been more fun I might have.

By far the worst amongst my section was the Policewoman. On good days she was sarcastic and snotty; on bad ones she was downright mean. She seemed to have a particular grudge against me and wouldn't even let me drive the car when we were teamed up together. She taught me nothing and enjoyed sapping my confidence. I dreaded having to work with her.

Despite this I was still full of enthusiasm for the job. It was certainly exciting, if nothing else. But more often than not it was my enthusiasm that got me into trouble.

I was on day shift a week or so after I'd started when we received a call about an indecent exposure that had occurred near some public toilets in one of Palmerston's inner-city parks. We had a good description of the offender and as the incident had only just happened we had a decent chance of catching him near the scene.

This was pretty cool. It's always good to catch a sex offender as they are the most reviled of all criminals and it feels great to get one off the streets. It also does your police credibility a world of good (and, god knows, I could do with some).

This particular offender was in his mid-teens and had a pushbike with him. As we were in a car we should have no trouble catching him, if we could find him. I was driving at the time and the young hoony cop was my partner. We cruised slowly around the streets surrounding the park, eyes peeled. Suddenly my offsider spotted the offender on the other side of the road.

'There he is!' he yelled into my ear, frightening the life out of me.

The young guy spotted us at the same time, jumped on his bike and peddled quickly away. I wrenched the steering wheel in a full arc and planted my boot on the accelerator, planning to do a quick U-turn in pursuit of the suspect. The car engine screamed and the tyres were smoking but for some reason we weren't going anywhere. I couldn't work it out - the car was in gear and the whole body was shuddering like it wanted to go forward. Then I realised what I'd done. I'd planted my foot hard on the brake at the same time as I'd slammed the other one on the accelerator. The excitement of the chase had rendered me incapable of remembering the basics of driving, i.e. the car will not go forward if you have your foot on the brake.

Realising my error I hastily pulled my foot off the brake causing the car to scream around at such high revs that instead of turning 180 degrees it turned 250 and we were left facing the footpath. By the time I'd turned the car the right way around, the suspect had got away. I felt stink but my partner was good about it, albeit confused. I told him the car had slipped out of gear but I don't think he believed me.

Fortunately the offender was caught later on that day. The complainant's description fitted a young guy who was well known to our youth aid section and they picked him up at home. He was intellectually handicapped and was prone to dropping his trousers on a whim.

Great. My first police chase and I'd been evaded by a handicapped teenager on a bicycle.

A chance to redeem myself came a few nights later while on late shift. I was by myself once again and was called to the Palmerston North Hospital where the nursing staff needed police assistance. One of their patients was a mite upset. This was probably because he'd had his face sliced open with a broken beer bottle and some dimwit doctor had shown him the damage in a mirror.

Normally the hospital would handle this sort of thing by themselves but on this occasion the patient was a very large gentleman who had lost it completely. He had grabbed a pair of scissors off a nurse and was threatening the staff with them. He was also very drunk and, I'd imagine, in a lot of pain from the wound. If that wasn't bad enough, he was also deaf and dumb, making it nearly impossible to communicate with him.

That's the scene I walked into. A large, injured, bleeding, drunk, angry, deaf and dumb Samoan, wielding a pair of scissors.

When he saw me he went berserk, brandishing the scissors in a threatening manner and knocking over a hospital tray in the process. I held my hands in front of me in a gesture of peace which calmed him down slightly but not enough for him to let go of the scissors. His eyes were as wide as saucers and I knew it wouldn't take much to tip him over the edge again. I wasn't surprised he lost it when he saw the cut. It was really nasty. The bottle had sliced him open from the bottom of one nostril right to the corner of his mouth and the cut was so deep his skin was flapping about like a fish's gill.

One of the doctors asked me what I was going to do. Good question. I had no idea. I said we needed to calm the Samoan down and asked if they had any tranquillisers. The doctor replied, rather sarcastically, we were in a hospital so they shouldn't be too hard to find. He sent a nurse off to prepare a hypodermic.

I asked for a pen and paper and tried writing a message to our enraged friend. I wrote 'Calm down, we are not going to hurt you' and held it up for him to see. He couldn't read. How the hell did this guy communicate with the rest of the world? Someone wondered if he knew sign language, he probably did - pity you couldn't say the same for the rest of us.

By the time the nurse arrived with the injections I had formulated a plan. I would approach the guy slowly, waving my hands in a placating fashion, then when I was close enough, and he'd calmed down (hopefully), I'd grab the arm he was holding the scissors with. From there I wanted the doctor and a couple of nearby orderlies to leap on him and help me hold him down while the nurse administered the sedatives. When I explained my course of action the doctor looked sceptical, but then that's what they are best at. It worked even better than I'd expected. By motioning to him gently and not approaching too quickly I gradually got his trust and even got him to put the scissors down. This was a relief as I hadn't fancied grabbing him while they were still in his hand. I even got him to sit on the bed.

By this stage I thought we might even manage the whole exercise without having to manhandle him but, at the last minute, he saw the injection kit and off he went again. This time I was close enough to grab him. So were the orderlies and we had no trouble pinning him to the bed while the nurse did her stuff. A few minutes later he was sleeping like a baby.

Once the drama was over I accepted the congratulations of the nursing staff and took my leave. I was so happy to have resolved the situation without anyone getting hurt I hadn't even considered arresting the guy. I could have charged him with threatening behaviour and a raft of other offences, but really, the guy had suffered enough and how the hell would I read him his rights?

The hospital must have phoned the station and reported on how I'd handled the situation because at the end of the shift my sergeant took me aside and told me I'd done well. I was rapt. Perhaps I could do this job after all.

My section must have thought I was getting cocky because they decided to bring me down a peg or two. This would take the form of an initiation prank. It was standard for new cops to have practical jokes played on them but you never knew when it was going to happen. There didn't seem to be any agreed time line and your initiation could happen at any stage within the first year.

Mine occurred in the first few weeks and, typical of my section, it was pathetic. All they did was have me drive around the around the airport at night, supposedly looking for a man with a shotgun. Half way through my search the hoony cop leapt out with a broomstick, giving me a mild start, and that was it.

Back at the station I heard tales of initiation pranks that had gone down in the annals of police lore. One such occasion involved a nervous young constable who was taken to the hospital morgue by his sergeant and asked strip the body of an old bloke who had recently died.

As they were about to remove the body from the freezer the sergeant was 'called away' on an urgent job. He instructed the new constable on how to remove the clothing from the body and then left him alone in the morgue. The young cop checked the toe tag to make sure he had the right corpse then pulled the body tray out of the fridge onto a waiting trolley.

Nervously he grabbed the sheet covering the corpse and pulled it back to reveal the badly shrivelled head of an old man. All of a sudden the corpse's eyes flicked open and the body sat up with a hideous moan. The startled cop did what most people would have done in similar circumstances and fainted, hitting the floor like a sack of spuds. He woke several minutes later to find his sergeant and other members of the Section rolling around the mortuary floor, laughing fit to bust. The 'corpse' had been another section member who had got an old man's mask from a fancy dress shop.

To me, the most alarming aspect of this story is that the practical joker was happy to be shut up in a fridge full of real corpses until his victim arrived.

Sometimes these practical jokes go wrong, as one did at the station where I was working. A young policewoman was working night shift and was put in charge of operations. This meant she was in the station by herself manning (womaning?) the phones. She was doing well, then, half way through the shift, three masked men burst into the control room and tried to tie her up.

Not realising they were her section members playing an initiation prank she treated the incident as real and fought like a demon. She got hold of her baton and swung it fiercely at one of the guys. He put up his arms in defence and the baton smashed into his forearm cracking a bone. She fought so savagely that one of the guys had to give her a hard shove just to get away. She tripped backwards over the chair and banged her head on the coms desk.

The guys quickly ripped off their masks to reveal who they were but it was too late, the damage was done. The policewoman was badly bruised and had a nasty gash on her head, while the attackers were cut and bruised with one nursing a broken arm. There was no way an incident of this magnitude could be kept quiet and when the Senior Sergeant found out there was hell to pay. The three assailants were put on a charge and she was commended for her good work. Fair enough too.

I was three weeks into my new job and still hadn't made an arrest. It didn't worry me but the rest of my section members were getting twitchy. There was no quota on arrests or anything like that but the party line was if you were doing your job properly then arrests would occur. This is true, but my attitude was arrest should be a last resort rather than an everyday part of the job.

Your first arrest is supposed to be a big deal but mine wasn't - it was more of an arrest by proxy. The offender was a student (in a university town, what are the odds on that?) and I arrested him for 'disorderly behaviour' as he was seen kicking over someone's front gate. He was drunk and relatively harmless, just stupid.

I was in the car when we picked him up and he admitted what he'd done under mild questioning. As I was there, and still an arrest virgin, they told me to arrest him. My entire contribution to the proceedings was to say 'You're under arrest' and to do all the paper work (in triplicate).

This included cautioning the offender, taking his statement and preparing his case for court the next day. I had two cautions to choose from, the short caution or the formal caution. I decided on the formal caution as it is so much more …. formal. It goes like this: Do you wish to say anything in answer to the charge? You are not obliged to say anything unless you wish to do so, but whatever you say will be taken down in writing and may be given in evidence.

Interesting to note that, unlike American TV cop shows, we do not say the evidence will be used against you. This is because we are nice Policeman and may use the evidence to help your case. Yeah, right.

The only other decision I had to make (in consultation with my sergeant) was what the actual charge should be. Technically he was guilty of wilful damage but that is quite a serious offence and as he cooperated with us we decided to stick with disorderly behaviour.

After arresting him, my next job was to hand him over to the watch-house keeper for processing. That done, I settled into the paper work, pausing only to reflect that I was now blooded - a real policeman with my first arrest under my belt. And even though it was only a pseudo arrest it still felt good to have done my job.

Much as I detested paperwork, I hated releasing prisoners from their cells more. This always happened on early shift – easily my least favourite rotation. What was to like? We started work at 5am and

235

I'm not a morning person. These days I'm disappointed if I'm awake in the 7's.

It wasn't just the obscenely early hour I found foul, it was the state of the prisoners. They had almost inevitably come in drunk, drugged or beaten up (not normally by the police), and frequently they stank. All of which made them grumpy. The fact they'd also been arrested gave them an excuse to behave like a sore headed bear but it was still not very pleasant.

Often the prisoners were disproportionately distressed about having their fingerprints taken. Most of them complained bitterly about getting their delicate wee digits all inky. This, from reeking, filthy guys who had recently urinated in their pants and had dried vomit matted in their hair. Go figure.

If early-shift prisoner release is one of the smelliest jobs in the police then scene guard has got to be the most boring. My introduction to it came during my second night shift. There had been a murder in the small nearby town of Foxton. A poor old lady had been knifed to death during a break in and the offender was still at large. The crime had been discovered earlier that morning and detectives had been working at the site the whole day.

A uniformed officer was required to be at the scene at all times, just in case the offender returned to dispose of any evidence he may have left behind. The detectives hadn't finished their crime scene investigation and Crusty and I were tasked to guard the location for the night. It was going to be a long shift as we were required there at 9pm and wouldn't be relieved until 9am the next morning.

The crime scene used to be a nice small-town home, but its charm had been destroyed forever by a brief violent act of cowardice. The big tough burglar had stabbed a 60-year-old woman seven times with a bread knife. I didn't know who he was but I hated him. I was half hoping he'd come back so I could have a crack at him; see how tough he was when he wasn't attacking an elderly woman.

I also feared his return. It was dark, the house was scary and I didn't really fancy copping a bread knife in the back. Oh well, at least I wouldn't be lonely. I had my colleague with me and we could engage in friendly conversation and perhaps even the odd laugh or two. This wasn't to be. He pulled rank as soon as the detectives left and threw me out of the car. He told me he was staying in the (warm and comfortable) vehicle while I patrolled the (cold and inhospitable) grounds.

He said he was going to have a kip and I wasn't to wake him for anything less than a sucking chest wound (at least I knew what one looked like). I was certain this wasn't standard police procedure but the withering glare I got when I mentioned as much put paid to further argument.

Before drifting off, my offsider informed me that the old adage of the criminal returning to the scene of the crime was based on fact. He also left me in no doubt as to what would happen if I let my guard down and got murdered. Having a colleague slaughtered created a lot of paperwork and he said if the offender didn't finish me off he would. I think these were just scare tactics to keep me on my toes. Although I did notice he locked all the car doors. I trudged into the cold, pulled my police greatcoat against my chest and hoped he had nightmares.

Once again it was just me and my, oh so vivid imagination. We weren't allowed to go inside the house as it had been sealed to protect the evidence. Which left me the outside, including a wooden front porch, to patrol. The veranda was the worst area because the front door had been left ajar, allowing me to see into the hall way where the body had been found. There were dark stains on the floorboards where the life had finally seeped out of the elderly lady. It gave me chills.

This was real. It wasn't an exercise carried out in the relative safety of Trentham. During training we were one step removed from reality. What we were shown and lectured on was either theory or it had happened to someone else. We were living those experiences vicariously. But now I was standing metres away from where a woman had been brutally slain, with the real possibility of the offender returning to the scene.

It was a long night with me jumping at shadows. But as dawn threatened my attention started to wander. By sunrise it had gone past wandering and was in the middle of a 20 kilometre trek. If the murderer had returned he could have whipped inside the house, mopped the hallway, done the dishes and a spot of vacuuming, repaired the porch and been on his way again without me even noticing.

This was one of my biggest problems in the police. I got bored easily and didn't pay any attention to detail. Jobs that required meticulous scene-searching and patience were beyond me. I quickly tired of what I was doing and wanted to move on to the next job, just missing that vital clue.

I've always been the same. My wife likened travelling around Europe with me to touring with a large excitable dog. After I'd been cooped up in the van for half a day driving, I had to be let outside for walkies and a good play.

Fortunately the offender didn't return and we were able to hand over a clean scene to the detective squad when they rolled up at nine the next morning. I say 'we' because my partner woke up at five to nine, due to some uncanny internal alarm developed through many years in the police, and greeted the detectives brightly, reporting all was well. He was as fresh as a daisy; I was knackered. Didn't stop the miserable git making me drive back to Palmerston though.

In a positive postscript to this story, if it's possible for such a tragic event to have an up-side, the offender was caught, charged and convicted for the murder. He was identified by a toe print discovered on a biscuit tin lid. He was 16 years old.

HE'S GOT A GUN

Sheep was amazed at my ability to sleep. He thought I could kip for my country. If the ability to catch zzzzs ever becomes an Olympic event, he claims I'd get gold. I think he exaggerates somewhat, though I admit to enjoying a rest as much as the next man, especially if the next man is Rip Van Winkle.

I think Sheep's judgement was coloured by the fact that he is a freak. I mean that in the nicest possible way, but the man was a machine. His baking job required him to be up to his arms in dough at ludicrous hours of the morning. His regular start time was 4am and often he'd be out drinking until 3am the night before, sometimes not bothering to go to bed at all.

I have never known anyone who could survive on as little sleep as Sheep. He was a bad influence on me and took me out drinking when I really wanted to be at home learning handicrafts.

After a week of late early shifts (1pm until 9pm the first day, then 5am til 1pm the next day), punctuated by late-night drinking and chatting with Sheep, was it any wonder I sometimes slept for 16 hours?

On occasion his lifestyle would catch up with him and some nights he'd sleep for four hours in a row. This is the same man who, in 20 years of working, has only had two and a half days off sick. And two of those days were used to drive to New Plymouth to buy a car off Carey's dad. That's taking dedication to one's work far too seriously if you ask me. Mind you, if I'd shown similar devotion perhaps I'd still be employed by Her Majesty the Queen.

To counter Sheep's sleeping super powers, I introduced the Cleanliness Of The Rooms Act. This cunning piece of legislation was designed to force Sheep to conform to Trentham-like standards of tidiness, with failure to do so incurring harsh penalties. The legislation was in effect for a week before Sheep gave up, paid the required amount of beer and tore the Act to shreds. Not that Sheep was particularly messy - beside me he was practically a saint - but he'd left home to get away from having to clean his room. Free from the constraints of Trentham, it wasn't long before I followed suit and the dirty washing pile in the corner of my room was a thing to be feared.

In my defence I soon discovered that not washing my clothes was only marginally less hazardous than washing them. We had a twin-tub washing machine and it was a beast. After having flooded the wash-house floor for the 50th time in a row I finally gave up and begged Carey for help. She obliged, not in the manner I'd anticipated (by doing my washing) but with lessons on how to use the washing machine properly. She was an excellent teacher and once I'd mastered the correct way to operate the poxy machine I only flooded the laundry every second time I used it.

I was used to having disasters in my private life and was trying hard to keep my Gonzoisms out of the work place. This meant keeping my head down at the station and I was happy just to make it through

241

my shift without fouling up. I also hoped to learn more about police work. Sadly, good teachers were thin on the ground. The guys that did care and wanted to help were often the younger guys, who were still trying to sort the job out in their own minds, so taking me under their wing was nigh on impossible. Besides, as I had no control over rosters, I had no choice who I was working with.

Most of the lessons you had to learn in the police couldn't really be taught anyway. Every situation was different and if you used your common sense (see earlier) you would normally come out of it okay.

The old adage, 'whatever doesn't kill you makes you stronger' was certainly true in the police and there was no teacher better than experience. This is an extremely good argument for not joining the police straight from school, as I had done. I knew little of the outside world. I had never travelled further than you can ride on a Kawasaki 100 (not far) and was unable to sort out my own personal problems let alone anyone else's. In many cases all I had to go on was what I'd learnt at Trentham; in others I had to wing it. Sometimes this worked, sometimes it didn't.

On one occasion a heady mixture of Trentham training techniques and pure dumb luck combined to give me a fleeting moment of glory, albeit at someone else's expense. That someone was my section sergeant who was, at the time, in charge of the public desk. We were on day shift and I was in the stationhouse preparing some paper work (just for a change).

At 2.20 in the afternoon an extremely large member of the

Mongrel Mob gang walked into the station. He was well known to the police and had a reputation as a guy not to muck around with. Rumour had it he was once seen walking to his car carrying three one-dozen crates of beer in each arm. Big, strong and mean - and on this particular day, not happy.

He'd been at the public desk talking to my sergeant for a few minutes before the commotion broke out. I heard the yelling and wandered down to see what the fuss was about. I arrived at the desk in time to see the huge bloke reach across the public desk and punch the sergeant smack in the face. The sergeant's nose exploded on impact and a fine spray of blood shot out as he keeled over.

'Holy Shit!' I thought. That's got to be against the law. And with little regard for my personal safety I launched myself at the enraged giant. Two other cops had also been drawn by the ruckus and they jumped on the big guy as well. The three of us piled into him, forcing him to the ground.

Even with a trio of cops grappling with him he was still bloody hard to contain. I had grabbed his left arm (figuring it was the least dangerous part of his flailing anatomy) and somehow bent it backwards behind his head. Whatever I was doing worked as he was still yelling a lot but unable to move much. I was very pleased about this. I had no doubt that he'd be biffing us about like rag dolls if we hadn't caught him by surprise, busy as he'd been turning the Sergeant's nose to mush.

Into this scene of blood and chaos came the senior sergeant, the officer in charge of the station at that time. He ran to where the four of us were thrashing about on the floor and offered us some handy advice.

'I think you should escort this man to the cells, constables.' he said in the kind of voice that implied we'd just been about to release the maniac with a caution.

'Oh great,' I thought. Now we're going to have to move him without dying in the process. Miraculously the savage beast had calmed down at the sight of the senior sergeant. The sergeant then appeared from behind the counter, came around to where we lay and stood on the Mongrel Mob member's head.

Looking at the sergeant's bloody pulp of a nose I can't say I blame him but he didn't make our job any easier. Unsurprisingly, having his head stood on enraged our captive and he started thrashing around like a madman again. I was hanging on as hard as I could, concentrating on keeping his arm locked behind his head. God knows how I'd got him into that position but it continued to work and when I pushed on his arm he yelled in pain and stopped struggling so violently.

Keeping a precarious grip on his arm we stood him up and dragged him to the cells. Every few steps he tried to have a go at us but my arm lock kept restricting him. Eventually we got him to the cell, threw him in and locked the door before he could rip us limb from limb. Once safely outside the cell all three of us staggered back to the watch-house and collapsed in a heap on the floor. We were knackered and covered in blood. Fortunately most of it was the sergeants, who had been rushed to the hospital by now. The senior sergeant came over to tell us what he good job we'd done. He singled me out.

'That was a very effective hold, Constable Wood.'

'Thank you, sir.' I replied hoping like hell he wouldn't ask me to show him how it was done. I had no idea, and couldn't have repeated it if I'd tried. He seemed happy though. He nodded and walked back to his office. That was the last compliment he ever paid me.

For the next few months work settled into a pattern. As I was still the youngest on the section I was rostered on the beat most of the time, especially during night shift. I didn't mind. I liked being on the beat. When you were in the cars you spent most of your shift being called to incidents, which was exciting, but meant running around like a mad thing and you'd always have heaps of paperwork to do at the end of the shift.

Being in the cars also meant there was a good chance I'd end up working with someone I didn't like, such as the hell bitch policewoman. A shift with her seemed to go on for ever, probably because she seldom deigned to speak to me and when she did it was to say something sarcastic. I tried to be nice for a while but that just seemed to antagonise her more. In the end we would just sit in silence. Eight hours is a long time to be in a car with someone who won't talk to you.

On the beat, I could do what I liked. Occasionally I'd be called to an incident within walking distance of the town square but not often. The rest of the time I was left to my own devices. If I was feeling brave enough, I would venture into the inner-city pubs. I didn't do this very often because there was more chance of running into trouble in the pubs and I discovered early in my career that I didn't enjoy confrontations.

This was something of a drawback, as a policeman's life is about 80 per cent conflict. Oh, I could handle the fights, the abuse and the arguments and I was more than capable of looking after myself. I simply didn't like that part of the job. A lot of cops did - they lived for it and were at their happiest when wading into a fight. Not me; if I could avoid trouble, I would. I enjoyed the part of policing where I felt I was doing some good, such as finding a kid who has been missing for a few hours, recovering stolen property, putting a bad guy behind bars, settling an argument through reason rather than violence. I liked happy endings.

My policing style meant I spent more time trying to prevent crime rather than solving it. After the pubs had cleared out I'd go around all the shops in the central city and make sure they were locked up and secure, then I'd poke about in dark alleys trying to catch out a burglar or prowler. Now, it's important to point out this is standard procedure for a beat constable. I don't want to paint myself as a shining beacon of goodness, single-handedly keeping Palmerston North safe from evil (if you've been paying attention I'd be amazed if you'd got that impression).

I was honest and well meaning and always tried to do my job to the best of my abilities. I was also lazy, lacking confidence and easily distracted. Quite often I would find myself a dark comfortable spot at the back of a picture theatre and hide there for a while watching the movie, scampering out just before the final credits. I also got to know the late night radio DJs and would pop up to the station to visit them when things got boring outside. I wasn't above finding a cosy spot for a bit of a kip on duty either. Hey - you try finding something to do in Palmerston North at 3am on a wintry Tuesday night.

More often than not beat was uneventful, although you never knew what was just around the corner. One night, it was my sergeant.

He'd just got back to work after his nose injury. Sadly the blow that smashed his nose also broke the camel's back. He'd had enough and decided to take early retirement not long after he got back to work. This made things extremely difficult for me. After the leadership I'd received from my sergeants at Trentham I found it discouraging to be working for a guy who wasn't interested in the job any more. He couldn't be bothered teaching me anything and was just working out his time. He wasn't nasty to me, he just wanted an easy life. With retirement plans to sort out his focus wasn't on the job.

This wasn't ideal. It was also dangerous.

On the night he picked me up from beat. We were the only ones available to attend a domestic dispute that had turned nasty. We received updated details while travelling to the address. We were told the woman involved had left the house and there was only a guy left in there, alone.

'Cool, hardly any reason for us to attend,' I thought.

He was upset and depressed.

'Diddums,' I thought.

He had a gun.

'Oh Shit.' I thought.

Surely the armed offenders would be called out. Nope, my sergeant and I were going to handle it. The guy didn't have a record and hadn't threatened anyone or fired his weapon so we were going to have a chat with him.

As has happened so often in my life I discovered that 'we' actually meant me. This became obvious when both of us arrived at the house and my sergeant waved me towards the front door, which was wide open. Sure, he was following behind me, but I was still going first.

Halfway down the front path we heard a shot from inside the house. This was not good. We beat a hasty retreat behind a fence. I was fairly sure he hadn't fired at us, as the sound was muffled and contained. The sergeant agreed and motioned for me to stay where I was while he headed back to the car. Assuming he would be calling for reinforcements I kept my head down and watched the front door. There was no sign of movement inside the house. Everything was quiet.

The sergeant returned quickly. He hadn't called for reinforcements; he'd gone to get his gun.

As you probably know, the New Zealand Police are not armed.

What you may not know is that all members of the police have ready access to guns. Revolvers are often carried in a locked box in the sergeant's car and other weapons are easily requisitioned if required. However, I should qualify this by saying that in my three years in the police I was only ever armed twice (not counting exercises or training). Disturbingly this was not one of those times as the gun was firmly in my sergeant's hands and he was not letting go of it.

Okay, I thought, at least that means he'll take charge and handle the situation. Wrong. He propped himself up on the fence, aimed the revolver at the door and motioned for me to go inside.

I hesitated, unable to believe what was going on.

'Don't worry,' he said. 'I'll cover you.'

Oddly enough I didn't feel particularly inspired by this. He was ordering me to go inside the house where an emotionally unstable, depressed man had recently fired a weapon, at God knows what, while he and his gun, stayed outside. That didn't seem very fair, or very safe.

Looking back it seems unbelievable I didn't even argue with him. But I was 19 and a rookie cop. He was my sergeant and I'd been given a direct order. It was a weird situation to be in. He was breaking every procedure I'd been taught when attending an armed domestic situation. But he was the sergeant in charge of the situation and it was his call. Trentham had conditioned me not to question a superior officer's orders, no matter how insane they might be.

I inched my way towards the front door, unsure who was going to shoot me first, the guy inside or my sergeant. All the lights inside the house were on and I had a clear view through the kitchen and into the living room. I couldn't see anyone. I was reluctant to move inside by myself and desperately wanted the sergeant to come with me. But he didn't move from the safety of the fence line and continued to wave me on. Fat lot of covering he'd be able to do when I was inside the house and he was still out in the garden.

I took a deep breath and crept into the house, keeping to the walls. I didn't know what to expect. The shot we'd heard earlier could have been anything - a misfire, target practice, a warning. Part of me hoped the guy had shot himself. That would be yucky and messy but at least it would reduce the chance of my developing unplanned new orifices.

The man with the gun was sitting on a chair in the lounge; his legs were thrown across the arm of the seat. He was very much alive and cradling a .22 rifle in his arms. A half drunk bottle of scotch sat beside the chair. An unlit fire rested in the hearth. The room was cold.

He didn't even seem to care about me. His head turned my way as I came in, then he looked away and continued staring at the wall. I was pleased to see he made no move to raise his gun, although he made no move to lower it either.

I didn't know what to do so I asked him if he was okay. He snorted and said not really. I mentioned the shot we'd heard earlier. He pointed to a bullet hole in the back wall and said that he'd shot the house.

Fair enough, I thought. It was his house, and it was highly

preferable to him shooting innocent young policemen.

I said I'd be happy to talk to him about whatever it was that was bothering him if I could have the gun. He shrugged and motioned for me to take it.

He offered no resistance as I took the gun out of his hands. I let out a sigh of relief and sat down next to him, trying to find out what was going on. After a few moments of awkward silence he opened up and began to talk to me. His wife had just left him for another man, which was obviously upsetting, but what was really getting to him was that she was entitled to take half of everything he owned. He told me he had worked really hard on the house while she was out spending his money and now she was forcing him to sell it. I knew this was only his side of the story but I couldn't help feeling sorry for the guy. I nodded a few times and commiserated with him, tutting about the misery heaped upon us by the many cruel and heartless harpies of the world. I even threw in a couple of 'Women, Boy's'.

I suddenly remembered the sergeant was still outside. His gun arm must have been getting mighty tired by now. I picked up the .22 and took it outside. My Sergeant seemed relieved to discover I hadn't been killed and I was pleased to note he had made some progress up the path. He was looking as if he might have made it inside, sometime in the near future. I explained the situation to him and he took the gun off me then put it in the boot of his car. We went back inside and picked up the house owner. The sergeant decided we should take him back to the station, where we could keep an eye on him. I agreed as the jilted dude was pretty depressed and was in no fit state to be left on his own. Besides, he had discharged a firearm in the suburbs, which was not ideal from a law and order perspective.

Firearm offences normally carry pretty stiff penalties but his situation didn't demand the full weight of the law be employed. We found a suitably lenient charge, arrested the guy and locked him up for the night. This allowed us to keep him under observation for the night then release him to friends the following morning, after he'd had time to mull over his actions. In our opinion the guy wasn't a menace to anyone but himself. He was seriously hacked off with his ex-wife but hadn't threatened her so we believed he didn't constitute a danger to her or to the public in general. In due course he had his day and court and because of the mitigating circumstances and as he had co-operated with the police (by not shooting me) he received a brief spell of community service.

It was a satisfactory result except for two things. The guy still lost half his house and I lost a great deal of respect for my sergeant. He had put me in a potentially life-threatening situation with little or no back-up. If the guy with the gun had flipped out I would have been stuffed. I lacked the experience to talk myself out of a hostage situation and the position my sergeant adopted outside wouldn't have afforded me any protection had the guy begun shooting. I didn't mention my concerns to anyone (except Carey) and I didn't dwell on the incident but it made me feel even more insecure within the section. The Sergeant retired a couple of weeks later.

This paved the way for a shake-up of my section. Some of the guys were leaving and several new faces were coming on board, including a new sergeant. The lucky candidate was to be announced within the next few weeks.

I was looking forward to having a new commander in chief. Perhaps a change in leadership would improve morale.

Even though I'd found my first few months in the police very hard, I knew, in some ways, they were also going to be my easiest. As a novice constable I'd been forgiven mistakes that would soon become unacceptable. My superiors had not yet caught on to the fact that I was a bad luck magnet and lacked common sense. My innate ability to fall over things had not yet surfaced and I hadn't given up trying to keep my uniform in tip top condition. I wasn't tired, disillusioned or sick all the time and the officers were yet to use me as a pawn in their political games. So, all in all, things weren't going too badly.

Which was lucky, as I was technically still on trial with the police. It took two years before a Constable received a permanent appointment and it is very easy to be thrown out within that period. Performance reviews were held every six months with your sergeant reporting on your progress. These reviews formed part of your permanent record and were used as a basis for your final selection. This would be tricky for me as my original Sergeant had left and I'd receive a report from a sergeant who had only known me for a month.

I wasn't too worried about this as I was determined to make a good impression on my new sergeant. I was still very enthusiastic about my career. The incidents I'd attended up to now had whet my appetite for action and I was keen to throw myself in boots and all. Yes indeed, my brilliant career in the New Zealand Police was like a flower about to bloom. Who would have thought there was a plague of locusts waiting just around the corner?

Nearly the end.

ACKNOWLEDGEMENTS

Thanks to Mum, Dad and Julie, for everything; and to Phil, Godfrey and Quentin for being brave enough not to change their names.

To all my police instructors, it wasn't your fault.
To Alix and Struan, Dave and Kerrie, Euan and Teresa and Maria, Eunice and Lisa, thanks for being my guinea pigs.

Thanks to Luke for the original cover and to Jimi for the new one - plus all your techy designy work.

And to anyone else I may have inadvertantly forgotten.

For god's sake Devon read it, you'll like it!

Printed in Great Britain
by Amazon

11375483R00150